LOW~FAT COOKING
ON THE GRILL

DELICIOUS MEAT, SEAFOOD & VEGETABLE RECIPES

FROM THE EDITORS OF TIME-LIFE BOOKS

TIME
LIFE
BOOKS

ALEXANDRIA, VIRGINIA

TABLE OF CONTENTS

Introduction *4*

Secrets of Low-Fat Cooking *6*

Chili Burgers

page 61

Poultry

Old-Fashioned Texas Barbecued Chicken *11*

Grilled Turkey and Orange Salad *12*

Barbecued Chicken with Tropical Fruit Salsa *15*

Dijon Chicken Kebabs *17*

Moo Shu-Style Grilled Chicken *19*

Grilled Cornish Game Hens with Apples *20*

Grilled Buffalo Chicken Sandwiches *21*

Grilled Chicken Fajitas *23*

Asian Chicken and Broccoli Salad *24*

Honey-Mustard Hens with Grilled Corn Salad *27*

Turkey Sausage and Pepper Heros *29*

Chicken with Red Chile Sauce *31*

Chicken Quesadillas *32*

Italian-Style Turkey Burgers *35*

Charcoal-Grilled Turkey Breast with Stuffing *37*

Chicken Souvlaki *39*

Spiced Cornish Game Hens *40*

Meat

Grilled Beef with Tomato Salsa *43*

Moroccan Lamb Kebabs *45*

Asian Grilled Pork Salad *47*

Grilled Beef with Squash and Mushrooms *48*

Beef Burgers with Basil and Mozzarella *50*

Marinated Flank Steak and Potato Salad *51*

Greek Lamb Kebabs with Mint Sauce *53*

Grilled Flank Steak and Vegetable Salad *54*

Steak, Mushrooms, and Onions Burgundy *57*

Grilled Spiced Pork Chops with Chutney *59*

Grilled Curried Beef *60*

Chili Burgers *61*

Grilled Pork Tacos *63*

Herbed Cheeseburgers *65*

Grilled Honey-Mustard Pork Chops *66*

Apricot-Glazed Beef Kebabs *69*

Southwestern Beef Salad *70*

Seafood

Shrimp Kebabs with Lime-Basil Orzo *73*

Grilled Trout with Fennel *75*

Sweet and Sour Halibut *77*

Grilled Scallops with Thai Noodle Salad *78*

Jamaican Jerked Shrimp with Pineapple *81*

Grilled Halibut with Fresh Tomato-Herb Sauce *82*

Herbed Flounder Rolls 83

Mixed Seafood Kebabs with Parslied Pasta 85

Grilled Tuna Salad Niçoise 86

Grilled Shrimp and Asparagus Salad 89

Striped Bass with Green Curry Sauce 91

Barbecued Salmon with Plum Sauce 92

Ginger-Soy Swordfish 93

Cod and Summer Vegetables in Packets 94

Barbecued Bluefish with Grilled Potatoes 97

Salmon Steaks with Pesto and Peppers 99

Salmon Burgers 100

Salmon Steaks with Pesto and Peppers

—

page 99

Vegetables

Mixed Vegetable Packets 103

Vegetable Burritos 105

Grilled Pizza 106

Grilled Eggplant and Feta with Pasta 109

New Potato and Pepper Salad 111

Grilled Vegetable and Mozzarella Sandwiches 112

Grilled Stuffed Mushrooms 114

Grilled Eggplant "Caviar" 115

Grilled Corn in the Husk 117

Vegetable Kebabs 119

Grilled Mushrooms, Potatoes, and Leeks 120

Grilled Red Onions 121

Grilled Carrot and Garlic Salad 123

Asparagus Parmesan 124

Grilled Peppers 127

Grilled Tomato Salsa 129

Grilled Potatoes and Sweet Potatoes 131

Grilled Butternut Squash 132

Desserts

Grilled Stuffed Peaches 135

Mixed Fruit Kebabs 136

Grilled Angel Food Cake with Chocolate Sauce 139

Hot Strawberry Sundaes 141

Double Chocolate S'Mores 142

Grilled Bananas with Rum Sauce 143

Open-Faced Plum Tarts 145

Apples with Apricot-Nut Stuffing 147

Grilled Pineapple with Orange-Maple Sauce 148

Grilled Pears with Butterscotch Sauce 151

Grilled Fruit Compote 153

—

Glossary 154

Index 157

Credits 159

Metric Conversion Charts 160

INTRODUCTION

Our mission in Low~Fat Cooking on the Grill *is to take the work and worry out of everyday low-fat cooking; to provide delicious, fresh, and filling recipes for family and friends; to use quick, streamlined methods and available ingredients; and, within every recipe, to keep the percentage of calories from fat under 30 percent.*

Grilling's soaring popularity shouldn't be surprising; countless delicious meals can be cooked with ease in the great outdoors while enjoying summer's long, languorous evenings. It's the best way to keep the kitchen cool in hot weather—and even the finest kitchen range can't duplicate the uniquely savory, smoky flavors of foods grilled over a fire. Gas grills make outdoor cooking a snap, and you don't even need to wait for warm weather to use them.

There used to be just two choices for the classic cookout: Hot dogs or hamburgers. Toasted marshmallows served as dessert. Today, there's much more to choose from, and fat-laden hot dogs will soon be a thing of the past when you have this book in hand: It's a treasure trove of innovative grilling ideas for meat, poultry, seafood, vegetables, and even desserts. Our chefs have come up with superb original recipes that feature surprising tricks for healthful, high-flavor grilling. Some entrées even have built-in grilled side dishes for the simplest meals ever.

SOMETHING FOR EVERYONE

The ever-popular chicken appears here in many guises. Our Poultry chapter will ensure that you never get bored with birds. Flavor-packed marinades take the place of sticky sauces, and poultry can be grilled with the skin to keep it moist. (As long as you discard the skin before eating, the fat is out of the picture.) There are succulent barbecues as well as festive salads; the Charcoal-Grilled Turkey Breast with Stuffing makes a fabulous nontraditional holiday meal.

You needn't deprive yourself of meat on the grill. The following luscious entrées (among others) are satisfying *and* low in fat: Marinated Flank Steak and Potato Salad, Moroccan Lamb Kebabs, and Beef Burgers with Basil and Mozzarella.

Delicate fish and shellfish may seem challenging candidates for grilling, but a grill-topper or grilling basket makes striped bass or scallops as easy to cook as steaks or chops, with spectacular results. The Seafood chapter includes recipes for swordfish and tuna—the two meatiest, easiest-to-handle fish—but don't hesitate to try Jamaican Jerked Shrimp with Pineapple or Grilled Scallops with Thai Noodle Salad as well.

These days we're all trying to eat more vegetables and less meat. Open to our Vegetables chapter (and welcome vegetarian friends) with such hearty dishes as Grilled Vegetable and Mozzarella Sandwiches, Grilled Pizza, or Vegetable Burritos. You'll also find pleasing "side orders" in this chapter, from colorful vegetable kebabs to classic grilled corn on the cob—yet more reason to get out of the kitchen.

When it's time for dessert, traditionalists will opt for our (lower-fat) Double Chocolate S'Mores. On a more inventive plane, there's also Grilled Angel Food Cake with Chocolate Sauce, Grilled Pears with Butterscotch Sauce, and much more. And what could be easier or more beautiful than summery Grilled Fruit Kebabs?

GRILLING BASICS

With this cookbook you won't be spending hours over the grill. Check the "Working Time" and "Total Time" for each recipe before you plan your menu, noting that the marinating time is additional (but since food marinates unattended, except for occasional turning, the marinating period is free time for the cook). Most of the recommended marinating times are flexible, although often the longer the food marinates, the more flavorful the result.

"Secrets of Low-Fat Grilling" (pages 6 through 8) will help you grill efficiently, safely, and, best of all, with unfailingly delicious results. So don't delay: Whether you have a hibachi or a capacious covered kettle, you're in for some truly special treats when you try these great grilling recipes.

CONTRIBUTING EDITORS

Sandra Rose Gluck, a New York City chef, has years of experience creating delicious low-fat recipes that are quick to prepare. Her secret for satisfying results is to always aim for great taste and variety. By combining readily available, fresh ingredients with simple cooking techniques, Sandra has created the perfect recipes for today's busy lifestyles.

Grace Young has been the director of a major test kitchen specializing in low-fat and health-related cookbooks for over 12 years. Grace oversees the development, taste testing, and nutritional analysis of every recipe in Low-Fat Cooking on the Grill. *Her goal is to take the work and worry out of low-fat cooking so that you can enjoy delicious, healthy meals every day.*

Kate Slate has been a food editor for almost 20 years, and has published thousands of recipes in cookbooks and magazines. As the Editorial Director of Low-Fat Cooking on the Grill, *Kate combined easy to follow directions with practical low-fat cooking tips. The result is guaranteed to make your low-fat cooking as rewarding and fun as it is foolproof.*

NUTRITION

Every recipe in this book provides per-serving values for the nutrients listed in the chart at right. The daily intakes listed in the chart are based on those recommended by the USDA and presume a nonsedentary lifestyle. The nutritional emphasis in this book is not only on controlling calories, but on reducing total fat grams. Research has shown that dietary fat metabolizes more easily into body fat than do carbohydrates and protein. In order to control the amount of fat in a given recipe and in your diet in general, no more than 30 percent of the calories should come from fat.

Nutrient	Women	Men
Fat	<65 g	<80 g
Calories	2000	2500
Saturated fat	<20 g	<25 g
Carbohydrate	300 g	375 g
Protein	50 g	65 g
Cholesterol	<300 mg	<300 mg
Sodium	<2400 mg	<2400 mg

These recommended daily intakes are averages used by the Food and Drug Administration and are consistent with the labeling on all food products. Although the values for cholesterol and sodium are the same for all adults, the other intake values vary depending on gender, ideal weight, and activity level. Check with a physician or nutritionist for your own daily intake values.

SECRETS OF LOW-FAT GRILLING

GRILLING

Grilling is a natural for tasty, low-fat cooking. Like roasting or baking, it's a dry-heat method, but since the food sits above the heat on a grill, rather than in a pan, any excess fat melts and drips off. Of course, the smoke of a charcoal fire is an unrivaled seasoning, so you enjoy full flavor along with reduced fat content. Our recipes make the most of these unique advantages, and you'll be happy to see that none of the dishes requires any particular grilling expertise or fancy equipment.

LOW-FAT GRILLING TIPS

If meat is the main dish, cut the fat by starting with the leanest cut available, then trim off any excess fat. The traditional way to keep grilling meat moist is to use a marinade or basting sauce that contains a fair amount of oil, but in fact oil isn't necessary: Our low-fat sauces and marinades will produce juicy, succulent results as long as you are careful not to overcook the meat. Cooking foods in a foil packet is another great way to seal in all the juices and flavors of grilled food.

PREPARING THE GRILL

The most basic requirement for successful grilling is a good fire. Gas grills are as easy and convenient to use as a kitchen stove; charcoal grills take

---

PREPARING THE GRILL RACK OR GRILL TOPPER FOR LOW-FAT COOKING

~

Most grill racks and grill toppers do not have nonstick surfaces. To reduce fat, our chefs use nonstick cooking spray (rather than oil) to prevent sticking. However these sprays, whether aerosol or pump, can cause flare-ups, so follow these steps for safety: Preheat the grill as directed; just before grilling, put on oven mitts, remove the rack or grill topper, and spray it with nonstick cooking spray. Carefully return the rack or topper to the grill.

---

a little more work. To build a charcoal fire: Stack charcoal briquets in a pyramid shape and saturate them with starter fluid, then light (never bring the lighter fluid can anywhere close to hot coals). Let the coals burn until the flames die down and the briquets are glowing but covered with white ash; this takes about 30 minutes. (Alternatively, start the fire in half the time without lighter fluid by using a chimney starter, shown opposite.) Use long-handled tongs to spread the coals before you start to cook. Grills come in many different styles, and heating instructions can vary considerably. Be

sure to read the manufacturer's directions for your grill before using it.

Our recipes express temperatures and heat as high and medium. Depending upon the type of grill you are using, you will have to adjust your heat source accordingly.

- **Gas grills:** Temperature control dials allow you to set your grill to the appropriate heat. Most gas grills need 10 to 15 minutes to preheat.

- **Charcoal grill:** Here's how to gauge the approximate temperature of your grill: Hold your palm 6 inches above the fire. If you can keep your hand there for only 2 to 3 seconds, your fire is hot; if 4 to 5 seconds, the fire is medium.

- **Broiler:** All of the recipes in this book can be cooked under the broiler. For recipes calling for high heat, place the broiler rack 6 inches away from the heat; for medium heat, 8 inches.

Burned-on food residues can ruin the flavor of the finest ingredients, so it's best to clean your grill after every use. After removing the food from the grill, close the lid to let residues burn off. Soak the rack (wrapping it in wet newspapers does the job well), then remove any remaining residue with a brass-bristled brush or crumpled foil and wipe dry.

EQUIPMENT

1 Chimney starter. Starts charcoal fires quickly without lighter fluid.

2 Butane spark lighter. Reliably produces a spark to light a fire.

3 Long matches. Provide extra safety when lighting a fire.

4 Mitts and pot holders. Should be well-insulated and flameproof.

5 Hinged grill basket. Secures food for easy handling on the grill.

6 Grilling tongs. Ideal for handling most foods on the grill.

7 Scissor-action tongs. Helpful for round foods like corn on the cob.

8, 9 Grilling spatulas. For lifting and turning meat. Top spatula has a serrated edge for cutting meat and a toothed edge for scraping the grill.

10 Wire brush with scraper. Used to clean the grill.

11 Long-handled fork. Good for turning and testing for doneness.

12 Long-handled basting brush. Has natural bristles that won't melt.

13 Basting brush. Used to brush on seasonings and marinades.

14 Wood skewers. For kebabs; soak for 30 minutes before use.

15 Metal skewers. The twisted shaft keeps food from slipping.

16 Grill topper. Great for small foods such as shrimp.

MARINATING

Marinating infuses food with flavor while helping to keep it moist on the grill. We've made creative use of low-fat and nonfat ingredients—herbs and spices, fruit juices, citrus zest, soy sauce, mustard, vinegar, tomato sauce, yogurt, chicken broth, ketchup, jam, sugar, and honey—along with small amounts of vegetable oil to produce vividly flavorful mixtures to enhance meat, fish, and poultry.

In some of the recipes, we use the same marinade twice—first as a savory advance seasoning, and later as a basting sauce to prevent moisture loss during grilling. We also use dry marinades, called rubs, which are mixtures of herbs and spices that can be massaged into meats to infuse them with flavor. The salt in a rub draws out just enough moisture from the meat to help spread the flavor of the seasonings and still keep it moist.

The secret to successful marinating is to make sure ingredients are evenly distributed to penetrate all parts of the food. We often marinate in a sturdy zip-seal plastic bag. To prevent spills and make cleanup easy, place the bag in a large bowl before filling it. After combining the ingredients, press the air out the bag and seal; leave the bag in the bowl. Turn the bag periodically to ensure that the food is thoroughly coated with the marinade. Alternatively, you can use a pan or bowl for mari-nating; glass or ceramic containers are best. Untreated aluminum pots or pans may react with acid in the marinade, causing the food to pick up a metallic taste or darken in color. Cover the pan or bowl to keep the aroma of the marinade from affecting other foods in the refrigerator.

Many of our recipes offer a range of marinating times. Don't hesitate to try a recipe simply because you don't have time to let it marinate as long as indicated. Even a brief marinating period —while you prepare the grill perhaps—will add some flavor. If you've marinated food in the refrigerator, bring it to room temperature before grilling. Otherwise, the food may cook unevenly.

Foil Packets	Skewers	Grill Topper	Foil Tent
	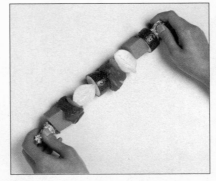		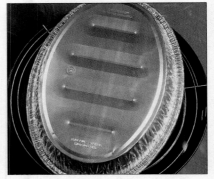

Foil Packets

Grilling packets should be made of double layers of heavy-duty foil to prevent tearing. To seal the packets, draw the short ends of the foil together; then roll the edges together, making a series of ½-inch folds. Leave the final fold up to act as a handle. Last, fold in or crimp the sides of the packet.

Skewers

If you have metal skewers, use them for grilling kebabs. When using wood skewers, wrap each end of the threaded kebabs with a small square of heavy duty foil. This will prevent the wood from scorching, and will create a makeshift handle for easy removal with long-handled tongs.

Grill Topper

To make your own grill topper, tear off a large piece of heavy-duty foil and fold it in half to make a double layer. Using a two-tined fork, make a series of holes over the entire surface of the foil. Use the punctured foil to cover the grill rack—before preheating—and proceed as directed.

Foil Tent

A grill cover keeps hot air circulating around the food, thus reducing cooking time and increasing smoke flavor. If your grill does not have a cover, you can use a disposable aluminum roasting pan, placing it over the food on the grill; remove it with oven mitts or long-handled tongs.

POULTRY

1

OLD-FASHIONED TEXAS BARBECUED CHICKEN

SERVES: 4
WORKING TIME: 20 MINUTES
TOTAL TIME: 45 MINUTES

*T*exans are quite serious about barbecue sauces: This pleasingly tangy baste is from the ever-popular tomato-and-vinegar school of BBQ. We add ginger for warmth and depth of flavor. The same sauce flavors both the chicken and the accompanying "baked" beans, and a cabbage-and-carrot slaw completes the meal.

½ cup plain nonfat yogurt

2 tablespoons reduced-fat mayonnaise

2 tablespoons cider vinegar

2 teaspoons Dijon mustard

½ teaspoon salt

¼ teaspoon freshly ground black pepper

1 head cabbage, shredded

4 carrots, shredded

3 cups no-salt-added tomato sauce

3 tablespoons firmly packed dark brown sugar

2 tablespoons grated fresh ginger

1 tablespoon red wine vinegar

2 cloves garlic, minced

Two 15-ounce cans pinto beans, rinsed and drained

4 whole chicken legs (about 2 pounds total), split and skinned

1. In a large bowl, combine the yogurt, mayonnaise, cider vinegar, mustard, salt, and pepper. Add the cabbage and carrots, tossing to combine. Cover the coleslaw and refrigerate until serving time.

2. Preheat the grill to a medium heat. (When ready to cook, spray the rack—off the grill—with nonstick cooking spray; see page 6.)

3. In a small bowl, combine the tomato sauce, brown sugar, ginger, red wine vinegar, and garlic. Place 1½ cups of the tomato mixture in a medium saucepan, add the beans, and bring to a boil over medium heat. Cook until the beans are coated and the sauce is slightly thickened, about 15 minutes. Spoon the beans into a disposable foil pan and cover with foil.

4. Grill the chicken, covered, turning occasionally and basting with the remaining tomato sauce, for 20 minutes or until the chicken is cooked through. Meanwhile, place the beans on the side of the grill for 10 minutes, or until warmed through. Serve the chicken with the coleslaw and beans.

Helpful hint: Make the coleslaw up to 8 hours in advance: The cabbage will become more tender and the flavors will blend and mellow.

FAT: 9G/17%
CALORIES: 474
SATURATED FAT: 1.7G
CARBOHYDRATE: 61G
PROTEIN: 40G
CHOLESTEROL: 104MG
SODIUM: 957MG

GRILLED TURKEY AND ORANGE SALAD

SERVES: 4
WORKING TIME: 20 MINUTES
TOTAL TIME: 55 MINUTES

1 pound small red potatoes

½ pound green beans, trimmed

¼ cup orange juice

2 tablespoons orange marmalade

2 tablespoons maple syrup

½ teaspoon salt

½ teaspoon ground ginger

½ teaspoon grated orange zest

¼ teaspoon freshly ground black pepper

1 pound boneless turkey breast, in one piece, butterflied

2 teaspoons Dijon mustard

1 tablespoon red wine vinegar

2 navel oranges, peeled and sectioned

4 cups red leaf lettuce

1. Preheat the grill to a medium heat. (When ready to cook, spray the rack—off the grill—with nonstick cooking spray; see page 6.) In a large pot of boiling water, cook the potatoes for 10 minutes to blanch. Drain. Tear off a 24-inch length of heavy-duty foil and fold in half to form a 12 x 18-inch rectangle. Place the beans and 2 tablespoons of water in the center of the rectangle and seal the packet (see page 8).

2. In a large bowl, combine the orange juice, marmalade, maple syrup, salt, ginger, orange zest, and pepper. Measure out ¼ cup of the mixture to use as a baste; set the remainder aside. Place the turkey on the grill and brush with some of the basting mixture. Grill, covered, basting and turning occasionally, for 30 minutes or until cooked through. Place the packet of beans and the potatoes on the grill next to the turkey for the last 10 minutes, turning the potatoes once, until the potatoes are cooked through.

3. Meanwhile, whisk the mustard and vinegar into the orange juice mixture remaining in the bowl. Add the orange sections, tossing to coat. Remove the turkey from the grill and thinly slice. Add to the bowl along with the green beans, potatoes, and lettuce, tossing to combine. Divide the salad among 4 plates and serve warm.

Helpful hints: Ask your butcher to bone and butterfly the turkey breast for you. Use a paring knife to peel and section the oranges.

FAT: 1G/3%
CALORIES: 337
SATURATED FAT: .3G
CARBOHYDRATE: 49G
PROTEIN: 33G
CHOLESTEROL: 70MG
SODIUM: 413MG

A butterflied turkey breast is textured like a thick steak, and when basted with this triple-orange sauce—made with orange juice, zest, and marmalade—it grills up deliciously juicy. Then, to create this elegant and flavorful salad, the turkey is sliced and combined with potatoes, green beans, orange sections, and a mustardy maple syrup and orange juice dressing.

Salsa
is not just tomatoes
and onions nowadays:
The creative and
crunchy sauce for this
tasty barbequed
chicken is packed with
mango, cilantro, and
pineapple. The natural
sweetness of the
tropical fruits is
ingeniously played off
against a touch of fiery
heat—supplied here by
cayenne pepper. And
the quickly marinated
chicken grills up tender
and juicy.

BARBECUED CHICKEN WITH TROPICAL FRUIT SALSA

Serves: 4
Working time: 15 minutes
Total time: 25 minutes plus marinating time

20-ounce can juice-packed crushed pineapple

1 mango, peeled and diced (see tip)

¼ cup chopped fresh cilantro or parsley

¼ cup chopped mango chutney

2 tablespoons fresh lemon juice

½ teaspoon salt

¼ cup ketchup

2 teaspoons olive oil

½ teaspoon dried oregano

¼ teaspoon ground allspice

⅛ teaspoon ground cloves

⅛ teaspoon cayenne pepper

4 skinless, boneless chicken breast halves (about 1 pound total)

1. Drain the pineapple, reserving ¼ cup of the juice. Transfer the pineapple to a large bowl and stir in the mango, cilantro, chutney, lemon juice, and ¼ teaspoon of the salt.

2. In a small bowl, combine the reserved pineapple juice, the ketchup, oil, oregano, allspice, cloves, cayenne, and the remaining ¼ teaspoon salt. Stir 1 tablespoon of the spiced ketchup into the pineapple-mango mixture, cover, and refrigerate until serving time.

3. Transfer the remaining spiced ketchup to a sturdy plastic bag. Add the chicken, squeeze the air out of the bag, seal, and marinate at room temperature for 30 minutes or up to 2 hours in the refrigerator.

4. Preheat the grill to a medium heat. Spray the rack—off the grill—with nonstick cooking spray (see page 6). Remove the chicken from the marinade. Grill the chicken, covered, turning once and basting, for 8 minutes or until cooked through. Cut the chicken into thin diagonal slices. Place the chicken slices on 4 plates, spoon the tropical fruit salsa alongside the chicken, and serve.

Helpful hint: Your best guide to choosing a mango is its fragrance. A sweet, slightly flowery aroma should be detectable at the stem end. If the fruit does not yield to gentle finger pressure, keep it at room temperature for a few days until it becomes softer and more fragrant.

Fat: 4g/11%
Calories: 332
Saturated Fat: .7g
Carbohydrate: 48g
Protein: 27g
Cholesterol: 66mg
Sodium: 705mg

TIP

Score each mango half into squares, cutting to, but not through, the skin. Turn the half inside out to pop the cut pieces outward. Cut the pieces away from the skin.

DIJON CHICKEN KEBABS

SERVES: 4
WORKING TIME: 15 MINUTES
TOTAL TIME: 35 MINUTES

If you're a fan of kebabs, good grilling skewers are a small but worthwhile investment. The shafts should have a twist to them, which helps keep the food from slipping. Serve these hearty skewered portions of chicken and vegetables with mesclun—a French-style mix of baby lettuces—or with a tossed green salad.

1 pound small red potatoes, halved

3 tablespoons honey

2 tablespoons Dijon mustard

1 tablespoon fresh lemon juice

½ teaspoon dried thyme

¼ teaspoon freshly ground black pepper

1 pound skinless, boneless chicken breasts, cut into 32 pieces

16 large mushrooms, stems removed

16 cherry tomatoes

1. Preheat the grill to a medium heat. (When ready to cook, spray the rack—off the grill—with nonstick cooking spray; see page 6.) In a large pot of boiling water, cook the potatoes for 10 minutes to blanch. Drain.

2. In a small bowl, combine the honey, mustard, lemon juice, thyme, and pepper. Add the chicken and mushrooms, tossing to coat well.

3. Alternately thread the chicken, mushrooms, tomatoes, and potatoes onto 8 skewers. Grill the kebabs, covered, turning occasionally, for 8 minutes or until the chicken is cooked through. Divide the skewers among 4 plates and serve.

Helpful hints: If honey has become crystallized in your cupboard, you can quickly re-liquefy it. Place the uncapped jar in the microwave and heat on high power for about 30 seconds.

FAT: 2G/6%
CALORIES: 305
SATURATED FAT: .4G
CARBOHYDRATE: 40G
PROTEIN: 31G
CHOLESTEROL: 66MG
SODIUM: 270MG

Moo Shu-Style Grilled Chicken

SERVES: 4
WORKING TIME: 10 MINUTES
TOTAL TIME: 20 MINUTES

Moo shu pork, a Chinese restaurant favorite, consists of stir-fried meat and vegetables flavored with Chinese hoisin sauce, served in crêpe-like pancakes. In our simplified grilled version, chicken is coated with a plum-jam sauce and Chinese five-spice powder and flour tortillas take the place of the pancakes. Garnish with a lettuce and radish salad and chopped fresh parsley.

8 scallions, trimmed

3 tablespoons reduced-sodium soy sauce

¼ cup plum jam

2 tablespoons plus 2 teaspoons reduced-sodium ketchup

2 tablespoons plus 1 teaspoon rice vinegar

¾ teaspoon five-spice powder

1 pound skinless, boneless chicken breasts

Eight 8-inch flour tortillas

1 red bell pepper, cut into thin julienne strips

1. In a large bowl of water, soak the scallions until ready to cook.

2. In a small bowl, combine the soy sauce, plum jam, ketchup, vinegar, and five-spice powder. Transfer ½ cup of the plum jam mixture into a measuring cup and spread onto the chicken breasts. Set the chicken aside. Using the remaining mixture, spread one side of the tortillas with the plum jam mixture and set aside.

3. Preheat the grill to a medium heat. Spray the rack—off the grill— with nonstick cooking spray (see page 6). Grill the chicken and scallions, covered, for 3 minutes or until the scallions are cooked through. Remove the scallions and cook the chicken, covered, turning once, for 5 minutes or until cooked through. Remove the chicken from the grill and grill the tortillas, jam-sides up, for 20 seconds to warm through.

4. Thinly slice the chicken on the diagonal. Dividing evenly, place the chicken, scallions, and bell peppers on the jam side of the tortillas. Place 2 filled tortillas on each of 4 plates and serve open face or rolled.

Helpful hint: You can substitute hoisin sauce for the plum jam, if you like.

FAT: 7G/14%
CALORIES: 435
SATURATED FAT: 1.1G
CARBOHYDRATE: 60G
PROTEIN: 34G
CHOLESTEROL: 66MG
SODIUM: 991MG

GRILLED CORNISH GAME HENS WITH APPLES

SERVES: 4
WORKING TIME: 20 MINUTES
TOTAL TIME: 40 MINUTES PLUS MARINATING TIME

Apple jelly, apple brandy, and cider vinegar make this an intensely fruity dish. Serve with steamed greens, such as spinach or kale.

¼ cup applejack or cider
¼ cup reduced-sodium chicken broth, defatted
⅓ cup apple jelly
3 tablespoons cider vinegar
1 teaspoon grated lemon zest
¾ teaspoon dried rosemary
½ teaspoon salt
½ teaspoon freshly ground black pepper
2 Cornish game hens (1½ pounds each), split
2 Granny Smith apples, cored and each cut into 4 thick rounds

1. In a small saucepan, combine the applejack, broth, apple jelly, vinegar, lemon zest, rosemary, salt, and pepper over medium heat and cook until melted, about 2 minutes. Set aside to cool to room temperature.

2. Place the hens in a sturdy plastic bag and pour half of the applejack mixture over them. Squeeze the air out of the bag, seal, and marinate at room temperature for 1 hour or up to 12 hours in the refrigerator. Meanwhile, place the apples in a shallow nonaluminum pan, pour the remaining applejack mixture over them and set aside to marinate at room temperature for 1 hour or up to 12 hours in the refrigerator. Turn the apples once or twice.

3. Preheat the grill to a medium heat. Spray the rack—off the grill—with nonstick cooking spray (see page 6). Remove the hens from the marinade. Grill, covered, basting with the marinade, for 18 minutes or until cooked through. Add the apples after 10 minutes and grill about 8 minutes, until softened but not mushy.

4. Place a hen half and 2 apple rounds on each of 4 plates and serve. Remove the skin of the hens before eating.

Helpful hint: Instead of applejack—an apple brandy made in America since colonial times—you can use Calvados, its French equivalent, or hard (fermented) cider.

FAT: 9G/21%
CALORIES: 386
SATURATED FAT: 2.5G
CARBOHYDRATE: 34G
PROTEIN: 36G
CHOLESTEROL: 108MG
SODIUM: 428MG

GRILLED BUFFALO CHICKEN SANDWICHES

SERVES: 4
WORKING TIME: 20 MINUTES
TOTAL TIME: 30 MINUTES

⅓ cup plain nonfat yogurt

2 tablespoons reduced-fat sour cream

2 tablespoons reduced-fat mayonnaise

1 ounce blue cheese, crumbled

½ teaspoon Worcestershire sauce

⅓ cup jarred roasted red peppers, drained and diced

1 rib celery, diced

1 carrot, diced

1 scallion, thinly sliced

2 teaspoons paprika

1 teaspoon dried thyme

¼ teaspoon salt

¼ teaspoon freshly ground black pepper

⅛ teaspoon cayenne pepper

1 pound skinless, boneless chicken breasts

2 tablespoons fresh lime juice

Four 6-inch pita breads

2 cups shredded romaine lettuce

1. In a medium bowl, combine the yogurt, sour cream, mayonnaise, and blue cheese. Stir in the Worcestershire sauce, red peppers, celery, carrot, and scallion. Cover and refrigerate until serving time.

2. In a small bowl, combine the paprika, thyme, salt, black pepper, and cayenne. Rub the mixture onto the chicken breasts, sprinkle the lime juice over, and set aside to marinate while the grill preheats.

3. Preheat the grill to a medium heat. Spray the rack—off the grill—with nonstick cooking spray (see page 6). Grill the chicken, covered, turning once, for 8 minutes or until cooked through. Slice the pita breads open along one edge. Place the pitas on the grill for 1 minute to lightly toast them.

4. Cut the chicken into thin diagonal slices. Dividing evenly, spoon half of the vegetable mixture into the pitas, top with the chicken and the lettuce, and spoon the remaining vegetable mixture on top. Place the sandwiches on 4 plates and serve.

Helpful hint: You can marinate the chicken for up to 12 hours in the refrigerator. Bring it to room temperature before grilling.

FAT: 7G/16%
CALORIES: 384
SATURATED FAT: 2.6G
CARBOHYDRATE: 43G
PROTEIN: 36G
CHOLESTEROL: 74MG
SODIUM: 757MG

Based on the famous "hot wings" created in Buffalo, New York, these sandwiches pair well with a cool salad.

21

GRILLED CHICKEN FAJITAS

SERVES: 4
WORKING TIME: 20 MINUTES
TOTAL TIME: 30 MINUTES PLUS MARINATING TIME

*F*ajitas—traditionally strips of skirt steak—are often made from chicken breasts, sliced either before or after cooking. Our tasty version has sliced grilled chicken (marinated in lime juice, olive oil, and chili powder), flour tortillas, shredded lettuce, and a zesty tomato-avocado salsa. Serve this Southwestern treat with a dollop of nonfat yogurt, if desired.

2 tablespoons fresh lime juice

1 tablespoon mild chili powder

2 teaspoons olive oil

½ teaspoon salt

¼ teaspoon freshly ground black pepper

1 pound skinless, boneless chicken breasts

1 pound tomatoes, coarsely chopped

4½-ounce can chopped mild green chilies, drained

½ cup chopped fresh cilantro

⅓ cup diced avocado

Eight 8-inch flour tortillas

4 cups shredded romaine lettuce

1. In a sturdy plastic bag, combine 1 tablespoon of the lime juice, the chili powder, oil, ¼ teaspoon of the salt, and the pepper. Add the chicken, squeeze the air out of the bag, seal, and marinate at room temperature for 30 minutes or up to 12 hours in the refrigerator.

2. In a medium bowl, combine the tomatoes, green chilies, cilantro, avocado, remaining 1 tablespoon lime juice, and remaining ¼ teaspoon salt.

3. Preheat the grill to a medium heat. Spray the rack—off the grill—with nonstick cooking spray (see page 6). Grill the chicken, covered, turning once, for 8 minutes or until the chicken is cooked through. Place the tortillas on the grill for 30 seconds to warm through.

4. Thinly slice the chicken. Place 2 tortillas on each of 4 plates, spoon the chicken slices onto the tortillas along with the tomato mixture and lettuce, and serve.

Helpful hints: If you prefer their taste, you can substitute corn tortillas for the flour tortillas. Rather than filling the tortillas before serving, arrange all the components on the table and let each diner create a personalized fajita sandwich.

FAT: 11G/23%
CALORIES: 438
SATURATED FAT: 1.8G
CARBOHYDRATE: 49G
PROTEIN: 35G
CHOLESTEROL: 66MG
SODIUM: 775MG

Asian Chicken and Broccoli Salad

Serves: 4
Working time: 20 minutes
Total time: 40 minutes

8 ounces linguine
⅓ cup orange juice
¼ cup reduced-sodium soy sauce
¼ cup chili sauce
2 teaspoons dark Oriental
sesame oil
2 cloves garlic, minced
½ teaspoon ground ginger
4 scallions, thinly sliced
2 carrots, shredded
3 cups small broccoli florets
1 pound skinless, boneless
chicken breasts

1. In a large pot of boiling water, cook the linguine until tender. Drain and transfer to a large bowl. In a small bowl, combine the orange juice, soy sauce, chili sauce, sesame oil, garlic, and ginger. Measure out ¼ cup of the orange juice mixture and set aside. Add the remaining orange juice mixture to the linguine along with the scallions and carrots, tossing to coat.

2. Preheat the grill to a medium heat. (When ready to cook, spray the rack—off the grill—with nonstick cooking spray; see page 6.)

3. In a large bowl, toss the broccoli with 2 tablespoons of the reserved orange juice mixture. Thread the broccoli onto 8 skewers. Brush the remaining 2 tablespoons orange juice mixture over the chicken. Grill the broccoli and chicken, covered, turning once, for 8 minutes, or until the chicken is cooked through and the broccoli is crisp-tender.

4. Cut the chicken into thin diagonal slices and transfer to the bowl with the linguine. Push the broccoli off the skewers into the bowl, tossing well to combine. Dividing evenly, place the salad on 4 plates and serve warm, at room temperature, or chilled.

Helpful hint: Dark sesame oil, made from toasted sesame seeds, is sold in Asian grocery stores, gourmet shops, and most supermarkets. Don't substitute light sesame oil—it is good for cooking, but does not add as much flavor.

Fat: 5g/10%
Calories: 445
Saturated Fat: .8g
Carbohydrate: 61g
Protein: 39g
Cholesterol: 66mg
Sodium: 945mg

You may recognize the flavors of Szechuan sesame noodles in this easy one-dish meal: The chicken, broccoli, noodles, and scallions are bathed in a mixture of soy sauce, aromatic sesame oil, garlic, and ginger. A touch of orange adds an original note. If you have Chinese noodles, you can use them instead of the linguine.

HONEY-MUSTARD HENS WITH GRILLED CORN SALAD

SERVES: 4
WORKING TIME: 20 MINUTES
TOTAL TIME: 40 MINUTES

Here is an all-on-the-grill meal—no stovetop or oven cooking is required. The corn is grilled on the cob for a superb smoky flavor, then the kernels are cut off and tossed with the same sweet-tart dressing used to marinate the hens. Garnish this with a fresh herb sprig and fresh lime wedges.

¼ cup fresh lime juice
3 tablespoons honey
3 tablespoons Dijon mustard
¾ teaspoon dried oregano
2 Cornish game hens
(1½ pounds each), split
4 ears of corn, husks removed
2 teaspoons olive oil
1 red bell pepper, diced
3 scallions, thinly sliced
¼ teaspoon salt

1. Preheat the grill to a medium heat. (When ready to cook, spray the rack—off the grill—with nonstick cooking spray; see page 6.) In a large bowl, combine the lime juice, honey, mustard, and oregano. Measure out ¼ cup of the honey-mustard mixture, lift the breast skin of the game hens, and rub the mixture underneath. Set the remaining honey-mustard mixture aside.

2. Brush the corn with the oil. Place the corn and the hens on the rack, and grill, covered, for 12 minutes, turning the hens after 9 minutes, and turning the corn occasionally until the corn is cooked through. Remove the corn and cook the hens for 6 minutes more, or until cooked through.

3. Meanwhile, holding the corn with a towel, cut the corn kernels off the cobs into the bowl with the reserved honey-mustard mixture. Add the bell pepper, scallions, and salt, tossing to combine. Place a hen half on each of 4 plates and serve with the grilled corn salad. Remove the skin of the hens before eating.

Helpful hints: When limes are inexpensive, buy a dozen and freeze them. After they've thawed, they'll be easy to juice. You'll need 2 medium or 3 small limes for the ¼ cup of juice required here.

FAT: 13G/26%
CALORIES: 441
SATURATED FAT: 3G
CARBOHYDRATE: 42G
PROTEIN: 40G
CHOLESTEROL: 108MG
SODIUM: 533MG

Turkey Sausage and Pepper Heros

SERVES: 4
WORKING TIME: 20 MINUTES
TOTAL TIME: 35 MINUTES

Inspired by the hearty sausage-and-pepper sandwiches featured at Italian street fairs, these heros (also called submarines, grinders, or hoagies), are packed with turkey sausage, peppers, and onions, all sizzling hot from the grill. The rich, heady tomato-basil spread slathered on the rolls is a unique addition: You'd never guess that its base is puréed kidney beans.

Two 8-ounce cans no-salt-added tomato sauce

¾ cup chopped fresh basil

2 tablespoons red wine vinegar or balsamic vinegar

½ teaspoon salt

1¼ cups canned kidney beans, rinsed and drained

10 ounces Italian-style turkey sausage, cut into 16 pieces

3 bell peppers, mixed colors, each cut into 16 pieces

1 Spanish onion, cut into 16 chunks

4 long Italian-style rolls (2 ounces each), split

1. In a small bowl, combine the tomato sauce, basil, vinegar, and salt. In a food processor, combine ½ cup of the tomato-basil sauce and the kidney beans and process to a purée, about 30 seconds. Set the bean mixture aside. Measure out another ½ cup of the tomato-basil sauce and set aside.

2. Preheat the grill to a medium heat. Alternately thread the sausage, bell peppers, and onion onto 8 skewers. Spray the rack—off the grill—with nonstick cooking spray (see page 6). Grill the kebabs, covered, turning occasionally and basting with the remaining tomato-basil sauce, for 10 minutes, or until the sausage is cooked through and the vegetables are crisp-tender. Grill the rolls, cut-sides down, for 30 seconds to lightly toast.

3. Place the rolls on 4 plates. Spread the reserved bean mixture on the cut sides of the rolls. Using 2 skewers per sandwich, push the sausage and vegetables off the skewers onto the rolls. Drizzle the reserved ½ cup tomato-basil sauce over the sandwiches and serve.

Helpful hint: Bell peppers for grilling should be thick-walled and meaty. Buy peppers that feel heavy for their size; they should be firm and glossy, free of black spots or wrinkles.

FAT: 11G/24%
CALORIES: 421
SATURATED FAT: 2.6G
CARBOHYDRATE: 59G
PROTEIN: 25G
CHOLESTEROL: 46MG
SODIUM: 937MG

The ruby hue of this chili-spiked sauce comes not from tomatoes (as you might expect) but from red bell peppers. The taste is unexpected, too—a complex blend of soy sauce, ginger, garlic, ground coriander, and chili powder. With so many flavors working for you, the simplest side dish will do: Steamed broccoli and grill-toasted pitas would work perfectly.

CHICKEN WITH RED CHILE SAUCE

SERVES: 4
WORKING TIME: 25 MINUTES
TOTAL TIME: 45 MINUTES PLUS MARINATING TIME

3 tablespoons reduced-sodium soy sauce

6 scallions, thinly sliced

4 cloves garlic, crushed and peeled

1 tablespoon chopped fresh ginger

1½ teaspoons chili powder

1 teaspoon ground coriander

½ teaspoon freshly ground black pepper

4 whole chicken legs (about 2 pounds total), split into drumsticks and thighs, skinned

3 large red bell peppers, halved lengthwise and seeded

¼ cup cider vinegar or rice vinegar

½ teaspoon red pepper flakes

½ teaspoon salt

2 tablespoons plus 1 teaspoon sugar

1. In a food processor, combine the soy sauce, scallions, 3 cloves of the garlic, the ginger, chili powder, coriander, and black pepper and process until smooth. Transfer the mixture to a sturdy plastic bag. Add the chicken, squeeze the air out of the bag, seal, and marinate at room temperature for 30 minutes or up to 12 hours in the refrigerator.

2. Preheat the grill to a medium heat. Spray the rack—off the grill—with nonstick cooking spray (see page 6). Grill the bell peppers, cut-sides up, covered, for 10 minutes, or until charred. Remove the peppers and set aside to cool slightly. Grill the chicken, covered, turning once, for 20 minutes or until cooked through.

3. Meanwhile, when cool enough to handle, peel the grilled pepper halves (see tip). Cut 2 of the pepper halves into thin strips and set aside. Add the remaining peppers to a food processor and purée. Combine the pepper purée, vinegar, red pepper flakes, remaining clove of garlic, and salt in a small saucepan and cook directly on the grill or on the stovetop over medium heat. Bring to a boil, stir in the sugar, and cook until the sugar has dissolved and the sauce is slightly syrupy, about 4 minutes. Stir the reserved pepper strips into the sauce. Place the chicken on 4 plates, spoon the sauce on top, and serve.

FAT: 8G/28%
CALORIES: 253
SATURATED FAT: 2.1G
CARBOHYDRATE: 18G
PROTEIN: 27G
CHOLESTEROL: 88MG
SODIUM: 824MG

TIP

The skin of grilled or roasted bell peppers can be removed easily by grasping the blackened skin and pulling it away from the flesh.

CHICKEN QUESADILLAS

SERVES: 4
WORKING TIME: 20 MINUTES
TOTAL TIME: 35 MINUTES

¾ pound skinless, boneless chicken breast halves

3 tablespoons fresh lime juice

Eight 8-inch flour tortillas

¾ cup shredded Monterey jack cheese (3 ounces)

½ cup chopped fresh cilantro (optional)

4 scallions, thinly sliced

½ cup mild or medium-hot reduced-sodium prepared salsa

1. In a small bowl, toss the chicken with the lime juice. Preheat the grill to a medium heat. Spray the rack—off the grill—with nonstick cooking spray (see page 6). Grill the chicken, covered, turning once, for 8 minutes or until cooked through. Remove the chicken and cut into thin slices.

2. Tear off four 24-inch lengths of heavy-duty foil, fold each in half to form a 12 x 18-inch rectangle and spray with nonstick cooking spray. Place 1 tortilla in the center of each rectangle. Dividing evenly, top with the chicken, cheese, cilantro, scallions, and salsa. Top with the remaining tortillas and seal the packets (see page 8).

3. Grill the packets for 5 minutes, or until piping hot. Carefully open each packet, quarter the quesadillas, divide among 4 plates, and serve.

Helpful hints: For a spicier quesadilla use pepper jack—Monterey jack cheese studded with jalapeños. You can also substitute white or yellow Cheddar for the jack cheese, if necessary.

FAT: 13G/28%
CALORIES: 426
SATURATED FAT: 4.8G
CARBOHYDRATE: 43G
PROTEIN: 31G
CHOLESTEROL: 72MG
SODIUM: 827MG

The Mexican version of grilled cheese sandwiches, quesadillas (queso means "cheese" in Spanish) are usually heavy on the cheese and on the fat. Here, a generous portion of lean grilled chicken—plus scallions, cilantro, and salsa—and a moderate amount of cheese transform this popular high-fat finger food into a deliciously substantial, but low-fat, meal.

Italian-Style Turkey Burgers

SERVES: 4
WORKING TIME: 20 MINUTES
TOTAL TIME: 30 MINUTES

*A*long with the more familiar turkey-burger ingredients—bread crumbs and oregano, parsley, Parmesan, and pepper—is one that will surprise you: club soda. It lightens the ground-turkey mixture so that the burgers cook up juicy and tender. For best results, handle the mixture gently, mixing it with two forks rather than squeezing it with your hands.

¼ cup ketchup

1 tablespoon balsamic vinegar

¾ pound skinless, boneless turkey breast, cut into large chunks

¼ cup Italian seasoned bread crumbs

⅓ cup club soda or seltzer

4 scallions, thinly sliced

⅓ cup chopped fresh parsley

¼ cup grated Parmesan cheese

½ teaspoon dried oregano

¼ teaspoon salt

¼ teaspoon freshly ground black pepper

1 red bell pepper, halved lengthwise and seeded

1 large onion, cut into ½-inch-thick slices

2 teaspoons olive oil

4 rolls (2 ounces each), split

1 large tomato, thinly sliced

1. In a small bowl, combine the ketchup and vinegar. Set aside. Preheat the grill to a medium heat. (When ready to cook, spray the rack—off the grill—with nonstick cooking spray; see page 6.)

2. In a food processor, process the turkey until finely ground, about 1 minute. Transfer to a large bowl and add the bread crumbs, club soda, scallions, parsley, Parmesan, oregano, salt, and black pepper. Mix until well combined and form into 4 patties.

3. In a medium bowl, combine the bell pepper, onion, and oil until lightly coated. Grill the burgers, bell pepper halves, and onion slices, covered, turning once, for 10 minutes, or until the burgers are cooked through and the vegetables are crisp-tender. Grill the rolls, cut-sides down, for 30 seconds to lightly toast.

4. Slice the pepper halves into ½-inch-wide strips. Toss the pepper strips with the onions and divide among 4 plates. Place a roll on each plate and top with a burger, tomato slices, and the reserved ketchup mixture, and serve.

Helpful hint: Balsamic vinegar, a product of Italy, is slow-aged in a succession of wooden casks for a mellow, sweet flavor. It's now sold in many supermarkets, although the finest balsamic vinegar—as pricey as Cognac—is available only at gourmet shops.

FAT: 9G/21%
CALORIES: 393
SATURATED FAT: 2.5G
CARBOHYDRATE: 48G
PROTEIN: 31G
CHOLESTEROL: 57MG
SODIUM: 958MG

CHARCOAL-GRILLED TURKEY BREAST WITH STUFFING

SERVES: 8
WORKING TIME: 40 MINUTES
TOTAL TIME: 1 HOUR 45 MINUTES

Roasted over indirect heat, this lavish entrée requires a good-sized grill. A gas-fired model will work if it has an indirect heat setting: Place the turkey in the foil pan and set the pan on the grill rack. Your butcher can flatten the turkey breast, or do it yourself using poultry shears to cut out the backbone, then pressing on the breast with your palm to flatten it.

1 bone-in turkey breast (about 6 pounds), split at the backbone and flattened
1 teaspoon olive oil
2 ribs celery, diced
1 large onion, chopped
1 cup sliced mushrooms
1 teaspoon dried sage
½ teaspoon dried thyme
1¾ cups reduced-sodium chicken broth, defatted
6 cups cubed whole-grain bread (about 12 slices)
½ cup chopped dried apricots
⅓ cup chopped pecans
¼ teaspoon freshly ground black pepper

1. Prepare a charcoal fire with the grill rack off. When the coals are ashen, divide them in half with long-handled tongs and bank them on opposite sides of the grill, leaving space in between. Place a rectangular foil pan in the space between the coals in the center of the grill. Place the rack on the grill, positioning it so that the handle holes are over the coals. Place the turkey in the center of the rack, over the rectangular foil pan. Grill for 1 hour 45 minutes, or until the turkey is cooked through, adding coals every 40 minutes.

2. Meanwhile, in a nonstick skillet, heat the oil until hot but not smoking over medium heat. Add the celery and onion and cook until the vegetables are softened, about 5 minutes. Add the mushrooms, sage, and thyme and cook until the mushrooms release their liquid, about 5 minutes. Remove from the heat and stir in the broth, bread, apricots, pecans, and pepper.

3. Tear off two 24-inch lengths of heavy-duty foil, and fold each in half to form a 12 x 18-inch rectangle. Divide the stuffing between the pieces of foil and seal the packets (see page 8). Place the packets at opposite ends of the turkey (not over the coals) for the last 45 minutes of the turkey's cooking time.

4. Remove the turkey from the grill and let sit 10 to 15 minutes. Thinly slice the turkey and divide among 4 plates. Serve the stuffing alongside. Remove the turkey skin before eating.

FAT: 7G/15%
CALORIES: 409
SATURATED FAT: 1G
CARBOHYDRATE: 28G
PROTEIN: 59G
CHOLESTEROL: 147MG
SODIUM: 434MG

CHICKEN SOUVLAKI

SERVES: 4
WORKING TIME: 25 MINUTES
TOTAL TIME: 30 MINUTES

The Greeks call skewered, grilled meats "souvlaki" and often cook lamb this way; chicken souvlaki is also popular. The chunks of meat are stripped from the skewers and served in pita pockets with a yogurt-cucumber sauce. Here, the cucumber is grilled with the chicken, onions, and tomatoes, and the sauce (made with nonfat yogurt) is flavored with mint.

1 cup plain nonfat yogurt
¼ cup chopped fresh mint
½ teaspoon salt
1 large cucumber, peeled and halved lengthwise
3 tablespoons fresh lemon juice
1 tablespoon olive oil
½ teaspoon dried oregano
¼ teaspoon freshly ground black pepper
4 skinless, boneless chicken breasts (about 1 pound total), cut into 16 chunks
1 large red onion, cut into 16 chunks
16 cherry tomatoes
Four 6-inch pita breads

1. In a small bowl, combine the yogurt, mint, and ¼ teaspoon of the salt. Set aside. Preheat the grill to a medium heat. (When ready to cook, spray the rack—off the grill—with nonstick cooking spray; see page 6.)

2. With a spoon, scoop out the seeds from each cucumber half and cut the cucumber into 16 pieces. In a shallow bowl, combine the lemon juice, 1 tablespoon of water, the oil, oregano, pepper, and the remaining ¼ teaspoon salt. Add the chicken, cucumber, and onion, tossing to coat. Alternately thread the chicken, cucumber, onion, and cherry tomatoes onto 8 skewers. Grill the kebabs, covered, turning occasionally, for 8 minutes or until the chicken is cooked through.

3. Halve the pita breads crosswise. Using 1 skewer per pita half, push the chicken and vegetables off the skewers and into the pitas. Place the stuffed pita halves on 4 plates, drizzle the yogurt mixture over, and serve.

Helpful hint: European cucumbers (also called hothouse or English cucumbers) would work well in this recipe, because they are firm-fleshed and virtually seedless. European cucumbers are usually about a foot long; so if you use them, you'll probably need only half of one for this dish.

FAT: 6G/14%
CALORIES: 397
SATURATED FAT: 1G
CARBOHYDRATE: 48G
PROTEIN: 37G
CHOLESTEROL: 67MG
SODIUM: 726MG

SPICED CORNISH GAME HENS

SERVES: 4
WORKING TIME: 15 MINUTES
TOTAL TIME: 45 MINUTES

***P**artner these hens and potatoes with sugar snap peas and cherry tomatoes sautéed in broth. Pierce the tomatoes first so they don't pop.*

1¾ pounds baking potatoes, quartered lengthwise

½ cup reduced-sodium chicken broth, defatted

2 tablespoons coarse-grained mustard

¾ teaspoon dried thyme

¾ teaspoon grated lemon zest

¾ teaspoon freshly ground black pepper

½ teaspoon salt

¼ teaspoon cayenne pepper

2 Cornish game hens (1½ pounds each), split

1. Preheat the grill with the grill topper to a medium heat. (When ready to cook, spray the grill topper and rack—off the grill—with nonstick cooking spray; see page 6.)

2. In a large pot of boiling water, cook the potatoes for 10 minutes to blanch. Drain. In a large bowl, combine the broth, mustard, and ¼ teaspoon of the thyme. Add the potatoes and toss to coat.

3. In a small bowl, combine the lemon zest, black pepper, salt, cayenne, and the remaining ½ teaspoon thyme. Lift the breast skin of the game hens and rub the spice mixture underneath. Grill the hens on the grill rack for 9 minutes. Turn the hens over, place the potatoes on the grill topper, and grill, covered, turning the potatoes occasionally, for 9 minutes or until the hens are cooked through and the potatoes are golden brown.

4. Place the hen halves and potatoes on 4 plates and serve. Remove the skin of the hens before eating.

Helpful hint: Vary the dish by trying it with different herbs. Some possible substitutes for the thyme are dried tarragon, dill, basil, and oregano.

FAT: 9G/21%
CALORIES: 390
SATURATED FAT: 2.5G
CARBOHYDRATE: 34G
PROTEIN: 40G
CHOLESTEROL: 108MG
SODIUM: 563MG

MEAT

2

Grilled Beef with Tomato Salsa

Serves: 4
Working time: 20 minutes
Total time: 30 minutes plus marinating time

Top round is one of the leanest cuts of beef, but it's delectably juicy when properly cooked. Here, the steak benefits from a lime juice marinade: The acid in the citrus tenderizes the meat. A fresh, chunky jalapeño salsa adds a lively counterpoint. Serve with a salad of Bibb or Boston lettuce, tomatoes, and radishes.

¼ cup fresh lime juice
½ teaspoon salt
¾ pound well-trimmed top round of beef, in one piece
¾ pound plum tomatoes, diced
½ cup chopped fresh cilantro or parsley
2 scallions, thinly sliced
1 pickled jalapeño pepper, finely chopped
Four 8-inch flour tortillas

1. In a sturdy plastic bag, combine 3 tablespoons of the lime juice and ¼ teaspoon of the salt. Add the beef, squeeze the air out of the bag, seal, and marinate at room temperature for 30 minutes or up to 2 hours in the refrigerator.

2. Meanwhile, in a medium bowl, stir together the tomatoes, cilantro, scallions, jalapeño, the remaining 1 tablespoon lime juice, and remaining ¼ teaspoon salt. Refrigerate until serving time.

3. Preheat the grill to a high heat. Spray the rack—off the grill—with nonstick cooking spray (see page 6). Grill the beef, covered, turning once, for 10 minutes or until browned. Let the meat stand 5 minutes before thinly slicing. Divide the steak and tomato salsa evenly among 4 plates. Serve with the flour tortillas.

Helpful hint: Plum tomatoes were used for this recipe because they tend to be dense and meaty. If plum tomatoes are not available, use round tomatoes: but halve them crosswise and squeeze out the seeds before chopping them.

Fat: 6g/21%
Calories: 254
Saturated Fat: 1.5g
Carbohydrate: 26g
Protein: 24g
Cholesterol: 54mg
Sodium: 544mg

Lamb *is tremendously popular in Morocco— served with couscous, it's practically the national dish. The traditional preparation of couscous requires a considerable amount of time; here, the quick-cooking couscous steams in five minutes and the lamb and vegetables cook quickly over the fire. Heat some pitas on the grill and serve them alongside.*

Moroccan Lamb Kebabs

SERVES: 4
WORKING TIME: 20 MINUTES
TOTAL TIME: 40 MINUTES

1 tablespoon fresh lemon juice

1½ teaspoons ground cumin

1½ teaspoons paprika

1 teaspoon olive oil

½ teaspoon cinnamon

½ teaspoon sugar

½ teaspoon salt

¼ teaspoon freshly ground black pepper

¾ pound well-trimmed boneless lamb loin chops, cut into 16 chunks

1 zucchini, halved lengthwise and cut into 16 pieces

1 yellow summer squash, halved lengthwise and cut into 16 pieces

1 red bell pepper, cut into 16 pieces

1 lemon, cut into 8 wedges

1¼ cups couscous

2½ cups boiling water

1. Preheat the grill to a medium heat. (When ready to cook, spray the rack—off the grill—with nonstick cooking spray; see page 6.)

2. In a large bowl, combine the lemon juice, 3 tablespoons of water, the cumin, paprika, oil, cinnamon, sugar, ¼ teaspoon of the salt, and the black pepper. Add the lamb, zucchini, squash, and bell pepper, tossing to coat. Alternately thread the lamb and vegetables onto 8 skewers, ending with 1 lemon wedge per skewer. Grill the kebabs, covered, turning occasionally, for 12 minutes or until the lamb is cooked through.

3. Meanwhile, in a large bowl combine the couscous, boiling water, and the remaining ¼ teaspoon salt. Cover and let sit for 5 minutes, or until the liquid has been absorbed. Fluff the couscous with a fork (see tip) and transfer to a serving platter. Place the kebabs on the couscous and serve.

Helpful hint: You can thread the kebabs up to 2 hours in advance and keep them refrigerated.

FAT: 8G/18%
CALORIES: 392
SATURATED FAT: 2.5G
CARBOHYDRATE: 51G
PROTEIN: 28G
CHOLESTEROL: 61MG
SODIUM: 337MG

TIP

Traditional North African couscous is fine-grained cracked semolina, which takes a long time and quite a bit of work to prepare. But the couscous found in supermarkets is a precooked semolina pasta that requires only steeping. Fluff the softened couscous with a fork, which will separate the grains without crushing them.

Asian Grilled Pork Salad

Serves: 4
Working time: 25 minutes
Total time: 30 minutes plus marinating time

Generous slices of pork in an irresistible citrus-sesame-ginger sauce are the focus of this splendid salad. There's a terrific timesaving trick in this recipe: The vegetables—jade-green snow peas and diminutive carrots—are cooked right along with the pasta (the peppers are grilled with the pork). The "baby" carrots come peeled, washed, and ready to use.

¼ cup reduced-sodium soy sauce
¼ cup orange marmalade
2 tablespoons frozen orange juice concentrate
1 tablespoon chopped fresh ginger
⅛ teaspoon ground cloves
¾ pound well-trimmed pork tenderloin
2 teaspoons dark Oriental sesame oil
2 tablespoons white wine vinegar
8 ounces linguine
2 cups peeled baby carrots
1 cup snow peas
2 red bell peppers, cut into 2-inch-wide strips
1 navel orange, peeled and sectioned

1. In a large bowl, combine the soy sauce, marmalade, orange juice concentrate, ginger, and cloves. Transfer ⅓ cup of the mixture to a sturdy plastic bag. Add the pork, squeeze the air out of the bag, seal, and marinate at room temperature for 20 minutes or up to 12 hours in the refrigerator. To the orange-soy mixture remaining in the bowl, add the sesame oil and vinegar. Set the dressing aside.

2. Meanwhile, in a large pot of boiling water, cook the linguine for 5 minutes. Add the carrots and cook for 6 minutes. Add the snow peas and cook until the pasta is tender, about 30 seconds. Drain the pasta and vegetables and rinse under cold water. Add the pasta and vegetables to the dressing in the bowl, tossing to coat.

3. Preheat the grill to a medium heat. Spray the rack—off the grill—with nonstick cooking spray (see page 6). Grill the pork and bell peppers, covered, turning occasionally, and basting with the marinade for 15 minutes or until the pork is cooked through and the pepper skins are blackened. (Remove the peppers before the pork if necessary.)

4. Slice the pork and divide among 4 plates. Add the peppers to the pasta and vegetables and divide the salad among the plates. Drizzle any dressing remaining in the bowl over the pork. Arrange the orange sections on top of the plates and serve warm or at room temperature.

Fat: 8g/15%
Calories: 490
Saturated Fat: 1.9g
Carbohydrate: 76g
Protein: 30g
Cholesterol: 60mg
Sodium: 679mg

GRILLED BEEF WITH SQUASH AND MUSHROOMS

SERVES: 4
WORKING TIME: 25 MINUTES
TOTAL TIME: 40 MINUTES PLUS MARINATING TIME

2 tablespoons chopped fresh rosemary or 2 teaspoons dried

½ teaspoon dried thyme

½ teaspoon dried sage

½ teaspoon salt

¼ teaspoon freshly ground black pepper

5½-ounce can spicy tomato-vegetable juice

2 tablespoons fresh lemon juice

¾ pound well-trimmed top round of beef, cut into 16 chunks

1 acorn squash, halved and seeded

2 small zucchini, each halved lengthwise and cut into 8 pieces

16 large mushrooms, stems removed

1. In a small dish, combine 1 tablespoon of the rosemary, the thyme, sage, salt, and pepper. Set aside. In a sturdy plastic bag, combine the tomato-vegetable juice, lemon juice, and the remaining 1 tablespoon rosemary. Add the beef, squeeze the air out of the bag, seal, and marinate at room temperature for 30 minutes or up to 12 hours in the refrigerator.

2. Meanwhile, in a large pot of boiling water, cook the squash until fork-tender, 12 to 15 minutes. Drain. When cool enough to handle, cut the squash into 16 pieces.

3. Preheat the grill to a medium heat. Alternately thread the beef, zucchini, mushrooms, and squash onto 8 skewers. Brush the skewers with the marinade and sprinkle with the reserved herb mixture. Spray the rack—off the grill—with nonstick cooking spray (see page 6). Grill the kebabs, covered, turning occasionally, for 10 minutes or until the beef is medium-rare.

Helpful hint: Instead of the acorn squash, you might try another small hardshell squash, such as Sweet Dumpling or Delicata, which can often be found at farmers' markets.

Assuming that the weather cooperates, you can go on grilling well into the fall (and even the winter). So when winter squash makes its autumn appearance, try these substantial kebabs. The beef cubes and vegetables are marinated with sage and rosemary—robust herbs that are just right for cooler weather.

FAT: 4G/17%
CALORIES: 212
SATURATED FAT: 1.2G
CARBOHYDRATE: 23G
PROTEIN: 24G
CHOLESTEROL: 54MG
SODIUM: 442MG

Beef Burgers with Basil and Mozzarella

SERVES: 4
WORKING TIME: 10 MINUTES
TOTAL TIME: 20 MINUTES

Prepare to open wide (or pick up your knife and fork) for these oversized, herb-fragrant burgers.

¾ pound well-trimmed bottom round of beef, cut into chunks

½ cup no-salt-added tomato sauce

3 slices (1 ounce each) white sandwich bread, crumbled

¼ cup low-fat (1%) milk

½ cup chopped fresh basil

½ teaspoon dried oregano

½ teaspoon salt

6 tablespoons shredded part-skim mozzarella

1 loaf of Italian bread (8 ounces), quartered crosswise and split horizontally

1. Preheat the grill to a medium heat. (When ready to cook, spray the rack—off the grill—with nonstick cooking spray; see page 6.)

2. In a food processor, process the beef until coarsely ground, about 30 seconds. In a large bowl, combine the beef and ¼ cup of the tomato sauce. In a small bowl, combine the crumbled bread and the milk, tossing to thoroughly moisten the bread. Add the moistened bread to the beef mixture along with the basil, oregano, and salt. Shape the mixture into 4 oval patties.

3. Grill the burgers, covered, turning occasionally, for 8 minutes or until browned and cooked through. Spoon the remaining ¼ cup tomato sauce over the burgers and sprinkle the cheese over. Cook, covered, just until the cheese has melted, about 30 seconds. Meanwhile, grill the Italian bread, cut-sides down, for 30 seconds to lightly toast. Place a piece of bread on each of 4 plates, top with a burger and a second piece of bread, and serve.

Helpful hint: Lovers of cold meat loaf sandwiches might like to plan for leftovers: The burger patties are great the second day, sliced and served on a crusty roll.

FAT: 10G/23%
CALORIES: 393
SATURATED FAT: 3.6G
CARBOHYDRATE: 44G
PROTEIN: 31G
CHOLESTEROL: 68MG
SODIUM: 816MG

MARINATED FLANK STEAK AND POTATO SALAD

SERVES: 4
WORKING TIME: 15 MINUTES
TOTAL TIME: 35 MINUTES

1 pound baking potatoes

¼ cup reduced-sodium chicken broth, defatted

1¼ teaspoons paprika

1 teaspoon dried thyme

½ teaspoon salt

¼ teaspoon freshly ground black pepper

2 cloves garlic, minced

¾ pound well-trimmed flank steak

3 tablespoons reduced-fat sour cream

2 tablespoons drained white horseradish

1 tablespoon distilled white vinegar

2 teaspoons coarse-grained mustard

½ pound plum tomatoes, coarsely chopped

2 tablespoons snipped fresh dill

1. In a large pot of boiling water, cook the potatoes for 10 minutes to blanch. Drain, then quarter the potatoes lengthwise. In a large shallow bowl, combine the broth, paprika, thyme, salt, pepper, and garlic. Add the potatoes and the steak and turn to coat with the paprika mixture. Set aside to marinate at room temperature while the grill preheats.

2. Preheat the grill to a high heat. Spray the rack and the grill topper—off the grill—with nonstick cooking spray (see page 6). Grill the potatoes on the grill topper and the steak on the rack, covered, turning occasionally, for 10 minutes or until the steak is medium-rare.

3. Meanwhile, in a large bowl, combine the sour cream, horseradish, vinegar, and mustard. Dice the potatoes and and add to the sour cream mixture along with the tomatoes and dill. Slice the steak, divide among 4 plates, and serve with the potato salad.

Helpful hint: You can marinate the steak for several hours or overnight in the refrigerator.

FAT: 8G/28%
CALORIES: 260
SATURATED FAT: 3.6G
CARBOHYDRATE: 25G
PROTEIN: 22G
CHOLESTEROL: 47MG
SODIUM: 425MG

Corn on the cob is the perfect accompaniment for this delicious steak and horseradish-spiked potato salad.

Greek Lamb Kebabs with Mint Sauce

SERVES: 4
WORKING TIME: 15 MINUTES
TOTAL TIME: 25 MINUTES

What appears at first glance to be rice is actually the grain-shaped pasta called orzo (the word means "barley" in Italian). Orzo is a favorite in Greece—so it's the perfect partner for these marinated lamb kebabs with mint sauce. Round out the meal with steamed green beans and diced carrots.

½ cup plain nonfat yogurt
⅓ cup chopped fresh mint
¾ teaspoon salt
½ teaspoon freshly ground black pepper
1¼ cups orzo
1 teaspoon olive oil
½ teaspoon grated lemon zest
3 tablespoons fresh lemon juice
2 cloves garlic, minced
1 teaspoon dried oregano
¾ pound well-trimmed boneless lamb loin chops, cut into 16 chunks
1 red onion, cut into 16 chunks
16 cherry tomatoes

1. In a small bowl, combine the yogurt, half of the mint, ¼ teaspoon of the salt, and ¼ teaspoon of the pepper. Cover and refrigerate until serving time.

2. In a large pot of boiling water, cook the orzo with ¼ teaspoon of the remaining salt until tender. Drain and stir in the remaining mint, the oil, and lemon zest. Set aside.

3. Meanwhile, in a shallow bowl, combine the lemon juice, garlic, oregano, the remaining ¼ teaspoon salt, and remaining ¼ teaspoon pepper. Add the lamb and onion, tossing to coat.

4. Preheat the grill to a medium heat. Alternately thread the lamb, onion, and cherry tomatoes onto 8 skewers. Spray the rack—off the grill—with nonstick cooking spray (see page 6). Grill the kebabs, covered, turning occasionally, for 10 minutes or until the lamb is cooked through. Divide the orzo among 4 plates, place 2 kebabs on each plate, and serve with the mint sauce.

Helpful hint: Rosemary is also excellent with lamb. For a change, try substituting it for the oregano.

FAT: 9G/19%
CALORIES: 435
SATURATED FAT: 2.6G
CARBOHYDRATE: 58G
PROTEIN: 30G
CHOLESTEROL: 61MG
SODIUM: 501MG

GRILLED FLANK STEAK AND VEGETABLE SALAD

SERVES: 4
WORKING TIME: 40 MINUTES
TOTAL TIME: 50 MINUTES PLUS MARINATING TIME

7 tablespoons balsamic vinegar

2 tablespoons plus 1 teaspoon Worcestershire sauce

1 clove garlic, minced

1 teaspoon dried thyme

1 pound well-trimmed flank steak

1¾ pounds small red potatoes, thickly sliced

½ pound green beans, cut into 2-inch lengths

2 bell peppers, mixed colors, halved lengthwise and seeded

2 tablespoons coarse-grained mustard

¼ cup apple juice

1 tablespoon olive oil

¾ teaspoon salt

4 cups torn leaf lettuce

1. Place ¼ cup of the vinegar, 2 tablespoons of the Worcestershire sauce, the garlic, and thyme in a sturdy plastic bag. Add the steak, squeeze the air out of the bag, seal, and marinate at room temperature for 30 minutes or up to 2 hours in the refrigerator.

2. Meanwhile, in a large pot of boiling water, cook the potatoes for 4 minutes. Add the green beans and cook until the potatoes are firm-tender, about 6 minutes. Drain and rinse under cold water; set aside.

3. Preheat the grill to a medium heat. Spray the rack—off the grill—with nonstick cooking spray (see page 6). Grill the steak and bell peppers, covered, turning occasionally, for 10 minutes or until the steak is medium-rare. Let the steak stand for 10 minutes before thinly slicing.

4. In a large bowl, combine the remaining 3 tablespoons vinegar, remaining 1 teaspoon Worcestershire, the mustard, apple juice, oil, and the salt. Add the potatoes, beans, and lettuce to the dressing, tossing to coat. Cut the peppers into 1-inch-wide strips and add to the salad bowl, tossing to coat. Divide the steak and salad among 4 plates and serve warm or at room temperature.

Helpful hint: For the tenderest slices, cut the steak across the grain, holding the knife at a sharp angle to the cutting board.

FAT: 11G/25%
CALORIES: 389
SATURATED FAT: 3.3G
CARBOHYDRATE: 49G
PROTEIN: 24G
CHOLESTEROL: 43MG
SODIUM: 677MG

Smooth balsamic vinegar and apple juice form the foundation for a delicious dressing: Using a mild vinegar means you need less oil to balance it, so the dressing stays low in fat. The flank steak also makes for a lean meal; take care, though, not to cook it beyond the medium-rare stage, as it tends to become tough.

STEAK, MUSHROOMS, AND ONIONS BURGUNDY

SERVES: 4
WORKING TIME: 20 MINUTES
TOTAL TIME: 30 MINUTES PLUS MARINATING TIME

*S*teak sandwiches are hearty fare, but these have an elegant aspect thanks to an herbed sauce made with red wine (inspired by the classic French dish boeuf bourguignonne). The creamy sauce, based on reduced-fat mayonnaise, tops layers of peppery greens, sliced steak, and grilled mushrooms and onions. Serve with a salad of leaf lettuce and radicchio.

½ cup dry red wine

1 tablespoon balsamic vinegar

1 clove garlic, crushed and peeled

1 teaspoon dried thyme

½ teaspoon salt

¼ teaspoon freshly ground black pepper

¾ pound well-trimmed top round of beef, in one piece

6 large mushrooms, stems removed

1 Spanish onion, halved and thickly sliced

3 tablespoons reduced-fat mayonnaise

2 tablespoons chopped fresh basil or parsley

1 loaf of Italian bread (8 ounces), quartered crosswise and split horizontally

1 cup arugula or watercress

12 cherry tomatoes, coarsely chopped

1. In a shallow bowl, combine the wine, vinegar, garlic, thyme, salt, and pepper. Add the beef, mushrooms, and onion and marinate at room temperature for 30 minutes or up to 2 hours in the refrigerator. Preheat the grill with the grill topper to a medium heat. (When ready to cook, spray the rack and grill topper—off the grill—with nonstick cooking spray; see page 6.)

2. Remove the meat and vegetables from the marinade and pour the marinade into a small saucepan. Place the meat on the grill rack and the mushrooms and onion on the grill topper and grill, covered, turning occasionally, for 10 minutes or until the meat is medium-rare and the onion is tender. Let the steak stand for 10 minutes before slicing.

3. Meanwhile, cook the marinade directly on the grill or on the stovetop over medium heat until reduced to a thick syrupy glaze, about 7 minutes. In a small bowl, combine the glaze with the mayonnaise and basil. Grill the bread, cut-sides down, for 30 seconds to lightly toast. Cut the mushrooms into ¼-inch-thick slices. Place 2 pieces of bread, open-face, on each of 4 plates. Top with arugula, steak, mushrooms, onion, basil sauce, and cherry tomatoes and serve.

Helpful hint: You can use French instead of Italian bread. French or Italian rolls would also work perfectly well.

FAT: 8G/20%
CALORIES: 363
SATURATED FAT: 1.9G
CARBOHYDRATE: 40G
PROTEIN: 27G
CHOLESTEROL: 54MG
SODIUM: 749MG

GRILLED SPICED PORK CHOPS WITH CHUTNEY

SERVES: 4
WORKING TIME: 25 MINUTES
TOTAL TIME: 45 MINUTES PLUS MARINATING TIME

*C*hutney, *a spicy-sweet fruit condiment, is most commonly associated with curries and other Indian specialties. But this unusual homemade chutney, rich with chunks of butternut squash, apples, and prunes, is delicious with simple spice-rubbed pork chops. Partner the chops with a mix of white and wild rice, topped with scallion bits.*

¾ teaspoon salt
½ teaspoon dried sage
½ teaspoon ground ginger
¼ teaspoon ground allspice
2 cloves garlic, minced
¼ teaspoon freshly ground black pepper
4 well-trimmed pork loin chops (about 4 ounces each)
¾ cup apple juice
2 tablespoons apricot or peach jam
1 tablespoon cider vinegar
1½ cups diced butternut squash
1 teaspoon curry powder
1 teaspoon ground ginger
1 Granny Smith apple, cored and cut into ½-inch chunks
½ cup coarsely chopped prunes
2 scallions, finely chopped

1. In a small bowl, combine ½ teaspoon of the salt, the sage, ginger, allspice, garlic, and pepper. Rub the mixture onto the pork chops and let stand at room temperature for at least 10 minutes (or up to 12 hours in the refrigerator).

2. Preheat the grill to a medium heat. Spray the rack—off the grill—with nonstick cooking spray (see page 6). Grill the chops, covered, turning once, for 12 minutes or until cooked through.

3. Meanwhile, in a medium saucepan, combine the apple juice, jam, vinegar, squash, curry powder, ginger, and the remaining ¼ teaspoon salt. Cook directly on the grill or on the stovetop over medium heat for 8 minutes. Add the apple, prunes, and scallions and cook until the apple and squash are tender, about 4 minutes.

4. Place the pork chops on 4 plates and serve with the chutney.

Helpful Hint: The same amount of dark or golden raisins, or finely chopped figs, could take the place of the prunes.

FAT: 4G/16%
CALORIES: 225
SATURATED FAT: 1.4G
CARBOHYDRATE: 38G
PROTEIN: 12G
CHOLESTEROL: 29MG
SODIUM: 445MG

GRILLED CURRIED BEEF

SERVES: 4
WORKING TIME: 15 MINUTES
TOTAL TIME: 30 MINUTES PLUS MARINATING TIME

The yogurt marinade tenderizes this steak and helps the curry and ginger flavors to penetrate it thoroughly.

¾ cup plain nonfat yogurt

1½ teaspoons curry powder

¾ teaspoon ground ginger

½ teaspoon sugar

½ teaspoon salt

1 pound well-trimmed flank steak

1 cup long-grain rice

2 cloves garlic, minced

1 small yellow onion, cut into ½-inch chunks

1 ripe banana, cut into chunks

2 tablespoons no-salt-added tomato paste

2 teaspoons fresh lemon juice

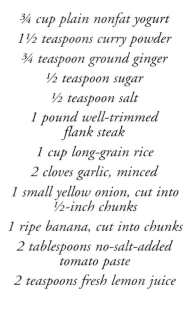

1. In a small bowl, combine the yogurt, curry powder, ginger, sugar, and ¼ teaspoon of the salt. Measure out ¼ cup of the mixture and set aside. Rub the remaining yogurt mixture onto both sides of the flank steak and set aside to marinate at room temperature for 30 minutes or up to 12 hours in the refrigerator.

2. Meanwhile, in a medium saucepan, bring 2¼ cups water and the remaining ¼ teaspoon salt to a boil. Add the rice and garlic, reduce to a simmer, cover, and cook until the rice is tender, about 17 minutes.

3. Preheat the grill with the grill topper to a medium heat. Spray the rack and grill topper—off the grill—with nonstick cooking spray (see page 6). Grill the steak on the grill rack and the onion on the grill topper, covered, turning once, for 10 minutes or until the meat is medium-rare. Let the steak stand for 5 minutes before slicing.

4. Meanwhile, in a food processor, combine the grilled onion, the banana, tomato paste, lemon juice, and the reserved ¼ cup of yogurt mixture and purée until smooth. Divide the rice among 4 plates, top with the steak and sauce, and serve.

FAT: 9G/19%
CALORIES: 421
SATURATED FAT: 3.9G
CARBOHYDRATE: 53G
PROTEIN: 30G
CHOLESTEROL: 58MG
SODIUM: 386MG

CHILI BURGERS

SERVES: 4
WORKING TIME: 20 MINUTES
TOTAL TIME: 30 MINUTES

1 pound well-trimmed top round of beef, cut into chunks

½ cup canned kidney beans, rinsed and drained

½ cup frozen corn kernels, thawed

½ cup chili sauce

2 tablespoons plain dried bread crumbs

1 egg white

2 teaspoons chili powder

¾ teaspoon ground cumin

½ teaspoon dried oregano

¼ teaspoon salt

4 hamburger buns, split

4 leaves of leaf lettuce

1. Preheat the grill to a medium heat. (When ready to cook, spray the rack—off the grill—with nonstick cooking spray; see page 6.)

2. In a food processor, process the beef until coarsely ground, about 30 seconds. Transfer to a large bowl. Add the beans to the processor and process until coarsely ground, about 30 seconds. Transfer the beans to the bowl and add the corn, ¼ cup of the chili sauce, the bread crumbs, egg white, chili powder, cumin, oregano, and salt, mixing to combine. Shape into 4 patties.

3. Grill the burgers, covered, turning occasionally, for 10 minutes or until cooked through. Grill the buns, cut-sides down, for 30 seconds to lightly toast. Place the buns on 4 plates and top with lettuce and a burger. Dividing evenly, top the burgers with the remaining ¼ cup of chili sauce and serve.

Helpful hint: Kidney beans have a "beefy" flavor, but you can use the same amount of another type of bean—pintos, for instance—if you have some on hand.

FAT: 7G/17%
CALORIES: 379
SATURATED FAT: 2G
CARBOHYDRATE: 42G
PROTEIN: 36G
CHOLESTEROL: 71MG
SODIUM: 986MG

Adding beans to ground beef gives you a deliciously thick but low-fat burger. Serve with a yogurt-dressed slaw.

GRILLED PORK TACOS

SERVES: 4
WORKING TIME: 20 MINUTES
TOTAL TIME: 35 MINUTES

For a change from crisp (fried) corn taco shells, try these soft tacos made with flour tortillas. Stuffed with grilled chili-marinated pork and onion, black beans, and avocado, these two-fisted tacos will satisfy the most serious of appetites—and nobody will guess that it's a low-fat meal.

4½-ounce can chopped mild green chilies, drained, juice reserved

¾ cup chopped fresh cilantro or parsley

3 tablespoons fresh lime juice, plus 4 lime wedges

½ teaspoon salt

¼ teaspoon ground ginger

⅛ teaspoon allspice

2 cloves garlic, minced

¾ pound well-trimmed pork loin

1 red onion, halved and thickly sliced

15-ounce can black beans, rinsed and drained

½ cup coarsely chopped tomatoes

4 scallions, thinly sliced

Eight 8-inch flour tortillas

¼ cup diced avocado

1. In a medium bowl, combine the juice from the green chilies, the cilantro, lime juice, salt, ginger, and allspice. Measure out 2 tablespoons of the cilantro mixture and set aside. Stir the garlic into the mixture remaining in the bowl and add the pork and onion, turning to coat. Set aside to marinate while the grill preheats.

2. Preheat the grill with the grill topper to a medium heat. Spray the rack and grill topper—off the grill—with nonstick cooking spray (see page 6). Place the pork on the grill rack and the onion on the grill topper and cook, covered, turning occasionally, for 10 minutes or until the meat is cooked through. Let the pork stand for 5 minutes before slicing.

3. Meanwhile, in a medium bowl, combine the green chilies, beans, tomatoes, scallions, and the 2 tablespoons reserved cilantro mixture. Place 2 tortillas on each of 4 plates. Dividing evenly, top with the bean mixture, pork slices, onion, and avocado. Roll up or fold the tacos and serve with lime wedges.

Helpful hint: You can marinate the pork and onion for up to 8 hours in the refrigerator.

FAT: 13G/24%
CALORIES: 479
SATURATED FAT: 3.4G
CARBOHYDRATE: 60G
PROTEIN: 30G
CHOLESTEROL: 50MG
SODIUM: 890MG

If you're wondering where the cheese is on this burger, look no further —it's on the inside. A blend of Cheddar and reduced-fat cream cheese is tucked into the middle of each seasoned beef patty before it's grilled. Add some crunchy pickle slices and a salad made with sweet yellow bell peppers to complete the meal.

HERBED CHEESEBURGERS

SERVES: 4
WORKING TIME: 20 MINUTES
TOTAL TIME: 30 MINUTES

¼ cup shredded Cheddar cheese

2 tablespoons reduced-fat cream cheese (Neufchâtel)

2 tablespoons chopped fresh parsley

1 tablespoon Dijon mustard

1 pound well-trimmed top round of beef, cut into chunks

2 scallions, thinly sliced

3 tablespoons plain dried bread crumbs

2 tablespoons ketchup

½ teaspoon salt

½ teaspoon dried rosemary

¼ teaspoon dried sage

4 hard rolls (2 ounces each), split

4 thin slices of red onion

4 slices of fresh tomato

1. In a small bowl, combine the Cheddar, cream cheese, parsley, and 1 teaspoon of the mustard. Set aside.

2. Preheat the grill to a medium heat. (When ready to cook, spray the rack—off the grill—with nonstick cooking spray; see page 6.)

3. In a food processor, process the beef until coarsely ground, about 30 seconds. Transfer the beef to a large bowl and add the scallions, bread crumbs, ketchup, salt, rosemary, sage, and the remaining 2 teaspoons mustard. Shape the mixture into 4 balls. Divide the reserved cheese mixture into fourths. Push one-fourth of the cheese mixture into the center of each ball (see tip; top photo), then pull the meat over the cheese to seal (bottom photo) and shape into burgers.

4. Grill the burgers, covered, turning occasionally, for 10 minutes or until cooked through. Grill the hard rolls, cut-sides down, for 30 seconds to lightly toast. Place the rolls on 4 plates, top with the burgers, sliced onion, and tomato, and serve.

Helpful hint: Instead of the Cheddar, you can use the same amount of Jarlsberg, Gouda, or Gruyère.

FAT: 11G/24%
CALORIES: 407
SATURATED FAT: 4.2G
CARBOHYDRATE: 38G
PROTEIN: 36G
CHOLESTEROL: 83MG
SODIUM: 942MG

TIP

Make an indentation in each hamburger ball and press the cheese-mixture into the center. Bring the meat together over the cheese and pat it into an even layer to seal in the cheese. Flatten each ball into a burger shape.

GRILLED HONEY-MUSTARD PORK CHOPS

SERVES: 4
WORKING TIME: 20 MINUTES
TOTAL TIME: 40 MINUTES

1¼ pounds sweet potatoes, peeled and halved lengthwise

3 tablespoons Dijon mustard

1 tablespoon honey

1 tablespoon cider vinegar

¼ teaspoon hot pepper sauce

¾ teaspoon salt

4 well-trimmed pork loin chops (about 4 ounces each)

⅓ cup reduced-sodium chicken broth, defatted

1 red bell pepper, finely diced

2 scallions, thinly sliced

3 tablespoons raisins

1. In a large pot of boiling water, cook the potatoes until firm-tender, about 12 minutes. Drain.

2. Meanwhile, in a large bowl, combine the mustard, honey, vinegar, hot pepper sauce, and salt. Measure out 2 tablespoons of the mixture and rub onto both sides of the pork chops. Set aside to marinate while the grill preheats. Add the broth, bell pepper, scallions, and raisins to the honey-mustard mixture remaining in the bowl, stirring to combine.

3. Preheat the grill to a medium heat. Spray the rack—off the grill—with nonstick cooking spray (see page 6). Grill the pork and sweet potatoes, covered, turning occasionally, for 6 minutes or until the pork is cooked through. Cut the sweet potatoes into cubes and add them to the honey-mustard mixture. Place the pork chops on 4 plates, spoon the sweet potatoes on the side, and serve.

Helpful hints: You can marinate the chops for up to 12 hours in the refrigerator. The sweet potato relish would work equally well with roasted chicken or grilled turkey breast.

FAT: 6G/19%
CALORIES: 288
SATURATED FAT: 2.2G
CARBOHYDRATE: 37G
PROTEIN: 19G
CHOLESTEROL: 47MG
SODIUM: 797MG

It's a shame to serve sweet potatoes only on Thanksgiving: They're delicious, and highly nutritious to boot. Grilling the potatoes brings out their natural sweetness, which is further accented by the honey-mustard dressing. Send the chops and potatoes to the table with steamed broccoli or Brussels sprouts and a lime zest garnish.

APRICOT-GLAZED BEEF KEBABS

SERVES: 4
WORKING TIME: 30 MINUTES
TOTAL TIME: 50 MINUTES PLUS MARINATING TIME

Even diehard meat-and-potatoes folks will go for these kebabs, packed from end to end with grilled chunks of steak, sweet potatoes, vegetables and—for a tangy counterpoint—apricots. The marinade is also apricot-based. White or brown rice, tossed with diced carrots and minced fresh parsley or mint, makes a fine side dish.

½ cup apricot nectar
¼ cup dry white wine
2 tablespoons honey
1 teaspoon grated lime zest
2 tablespoons fresh lime juice
1 clove garlic, minced
1 teaspoon dried oregano
1 pound well-trimmed bottom round of beef, cut into 1-inch cubes
16 dried apricot halves
¾ pound sweet potatoes, peeled and cut into 16 chunks
8 small white onions, halved
1 zucchini, cut into 16 pieces

1. In a sturdy plastic bag, combine the apricot nectar, wine, honey, lime zest, lime juice, garlic, and oregano. Add the beef and apricots, squeeze the air out of the bag, seal, and marinate at room temperature for 30 minutes or up to 12 hours in the refrigerator.

2. Meanwhile, in a large pot of boiling water, cook the sweet potatoes and onions until the potatoes are firm-tender, about 8 minutes. Drain.

3. Preheat the grill to a medium heat. Alternately thread the beef, apricots, onions, sweet potatoes, and zucchini onto 8 skewers. Spray the rack—off the grill—with nonstick cooking spray (see page 6). Grill the kebabs, covered, turning occasionally, and basting with the marinade, for 12 to 15 minutes or until the beef is cooked through.

Helpful hint: You can substitute apple juice or chicken stock for the wine if you like.

FAT: 6G/17%
CALORIES: 310
SATURATED FAT: 1.8G
CARBOHYDRATE: 41G
PROTEIN: 23G
CHOLESTEROL: 61MG
SODIUM: 48MG

SOUTHWESTERN BEEF SALAD

SERVES: 4
WORKING TIME: 25 MINUTES
TOTAL TIME: 35 MINUTES

There's true Tex-Mex taste in this summery salad— from cumin and coriander to tequila and lime juice.

¾ cup reduced-sodium tomato-vegetable juice

¼ cup fresh lime juice

1 teaspoon olive oil

1 tablespoon tequila (optional)

2 teaspoons ground coriander

1½ teaspoons ground cumin

¾ teaspoon grated orange zest

½ teaspoon salt

½ teaspoon freshly ground black pepper

½ teaspoon hot pepper sauce

1 pound well-trimmed flank steak

4 ears of corn, husks removed

1 red onion, halved and cut into ¼-inch-thick slices

8 plum tomatoes, quartered

3 cups Boston lettuce leaves

16 nonfat tortilla chips

1. Preheat the grill with the grill topper to a medium heat. (When ready to cook, spray the rack and grill topper—off the grill—with nonstick cooking spray; see page 6.)

2. Meanwhile, in a large bowl, combine the tomato-vegetable juice, 1 tablespoon of the lime juice, and the oil. Set aside. In a shallow bowl, combine the remaining 3 tablespoons lime juice, the tequila, coriander, cumin, orange zest, salt, black pepper, and hot pepper sauce. Set aside 1 tablespoon of the mixture. Add the steak to the bowl, turning to coat. Brush the reserved 1 tablespoon of spice mixture onto the corn.

3. Place the meat and corn on the rack and the onion and tomatoes on the grill topper. Grill the onion and tomatoes, covered, for 5 minutes or until the onion is crisp-tender. Grill the meat and corn, covered, for 8 minutes or until the meat is cooked through. Transfer the onion and tomatoes to the tomato-vegetable juice mixture. Transfer the steak to a plate, let stand for 10 minutes, and thinly slice. When the corn is cool enough to handle, scrape the kernels from the cobs and add to the onion and tomatoes.

4. Add the sliced beef (and any juices that have accumulated on the plate) to the bowl. Add the lettuce, tossing to combine. Place 4 tortilla chips on each plate, top with the salad, and serve warm or at room temperature.

FAT: 10G/27%
CALORIES: 336
SATURATED FAT: 3.2G
CARBOHYDRATE: 42G
PROTEIN: 25G
CHOLESTEROL: 43MG
SODIUM: 441MG

SEAFOOD

3

Shrimp Kebabs with Lime-Basil Orzo

SERVES: 4
WORKING TIME: 15 MINUTES
TOTAL TIME: 20 MINUTES

Shrimp is a snap to cook, and it always find an appreciative audience. The lime slices flavor the shrimp; discard them before eating. To serve this meal in a slightly more formal fashion, use fettuccine instead of orzo, remove the shrimp and vegetables from the skewers, and arrange them over the hot pasta.

3 tablespoons fresh lime juice
¼ cup chopped fresh parsley
1 tablespoon olive oil
2 cloves garlic, minced
½ teaspoon dried oregano
¾ teaspoon salt
24 large shrimp (about
1 pound), shelled and deveined
1 large onion, cut into
16 chunks
8 ounces orzo pasta
½ teaspoon grated lime zest
¼ cup chopped fresh basil
16 cherry tomatoes
16 very thin lime slices
1 green bell pepper, cut into
16 pieces

1. In a large bowl, combine the lime juice, parsley, 2 teaspoons of the oil, the garlic, oregano, and ¼ teaspoon of the salt. Add the shrimp and onion, tossing to coat. Set aside to marinate while you preheat the grill and prepare the orzo.

2. Preheat the grill to a medium heat. (When ready to cook, spray the rack—off the grill—with nonstick cooking spray; see page 6.)

3. In a medium pot of boiling water, cook the orzo until just tender. Drain, transfer to a large bowl, and stir in the remaining 1 teaspoon oil, the lime zest, remaining ½ teaspoon salt, and the basil. Cover loosely to keep warm.

4. Alternately thread the shrimp, onion, tomatoes, lime slices, and bell pepper onto 8 skewers. Grill the kebabs, covered, turning once, for 4 minutes or until the shrimp are just opaque. Divide the orzo among 4 plates, place 2 skewers on each plate, and serve.

Helpful hints: You can marinate the shrimp for up to 1 hour, if you like. To shell fresh shrimp, pull apart the shell at the belly end of the shrimp with your fingers, splitting the shell, and remove. We've left the tails on, but you can remove them if you prefer.

FAT: 6G/14%
CALORIES: 393
SATURATED FAT: .9G
CARBOHYDRATE: 57G
PROTEIN: 28G
CHOLESTEROL: 140MG
SODIUM: 560MG

Whole fish (typically sea bass) grilled with fennel is a specialty of Provence. Here, toasted and ground fennel seeds go into a garlicky orange and tomato based seasoning paste that's spread inside these whole trout. Accompany the fish with steamed vegetables and grilled new potatoes.

GRILLED TROUT WITH FENNEL

SERVES: 4
WORKING TIME: 20 MINUTES
TOTAL TIME: 35 MINUTES

1 tablespoon fennel seeds
½ cup chopped fresh parsley
3 tablespoons orange juice
3 tablespoons no-salt-added tomato paste
2 cloves garlic, minced
2 teaspoons grated orange zest
½ teaspoon dried tarragon
4 whole rainbow trout (10 ounces each)
2 tablespoons dry white wine
½ teaspoon salt
¼ teaspoon freshly ground black pepper

1. Preheat the grill with the grill topper to a medium heat. (When ready to cook, spray the grill topper—off the grill—with nonstick cooking spray; see page 6.)

2. Meanwhile, in a small skillet, toast the fennel seeds over medium heat, shaking the pan, until golden and fragrant, 1 to 2 minutes. Transfer the seeds to a spice grinder or food processor and process until ground to a powder. Place the ground fennel in a small bowl and add the parsley, orange juice, tomato paste, garlic, orange zest, and tarragon, tossing to combine.

3. Dividing evenly, spread half of the herb-tomato paste mixture into the cavity of each trout (see tip; top photo). Make 4 diagonal slashes on each side of the trout (middle photo). Sprinkle with the wine (bottom photo), then the salt and pepper. Place the trout on the grill topper and grill, covered, turning once, for 12 minutes or until the trout is opaque at its thickest point. Serve hot.

Helpful hints: For this recipe, purchase "drawn" fish, which means fish that has been scaled and gutted and is ready to cook. If you frequently grill fish, you might want a buy a special long-handled, fish-shaped basket that holds a whole fish securely, making it easy to turn.

FAT: 7G/24%
CALORIES: 262
SATURATED FAT: 1.3G
CARBOHYDRATE: 6G
PROTEIN: 41G
CHOLESTEROL: 110MG
SODIUM: 339MG

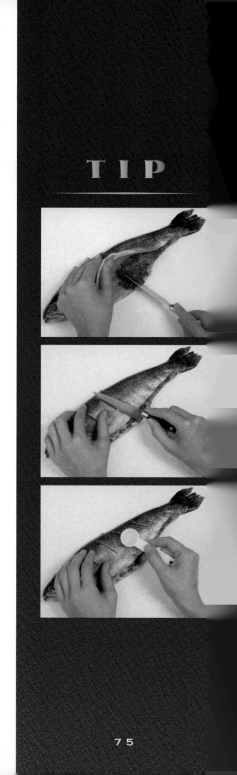

TIP

Sweet and Sour Halibut

SERVES: 4
WORKING TIME: 15 MINUTES
TOTAL TIME: 30 MINUTES

Despite its exotic flavor, the piquant marinade for the fish in this recipe is made with ingredients that you may already have on hand. If you don't already have rice vinegar, it's worth buying—it's extremely mild, allowing you to make dressings and marinades with very little oil. Serve the halibut with rice seasoned with lemon zest and fresh herbs, and a green salad.

¼ cup firmly packed light brown sugar

3 tablespoons rice vinegar or cider vinegar

3 tablespoons ketchup

1 tablespoon reduced-sodium soy sauce

1 clove garlic, minced

¾ teaspoon ground ginger

4 halibut steaks (about 1½ pounds total)

1 red bell pepper, halved lengthwise and seeded

1 green bell pepper, halved lengthwise and seeded

2 scallions, cut into 2-inch julienne strips

1. Preheat the grill to a medium heat. (When ready to cook, spray the rack—off the grill—with nonstick cooking spray; see page 6.)

2. In a nonaluminum pan or large shallow bowl, combine the brown sugar, ¼ cup of water, the vinegar, ketchup, soy sauce, garlic, and ginger. Measure out ¼ cup of the mixture and set aside. Add the halibut to the mixture remaining in the pan, turning to coat.

3. Grill the bell pepper halves, cut-sides up, for 5 minutes, or until the skin is blackened. When cool enough to handle, peel the peppers and cut them into thin strips.

4. Grill the halibut, covered, turning once, for 5 minutes or until the halibut is just opaque. Place the halibut on 4 plates, top with the reserved brown sugar mixture, the bell pepper strips, and the scallions, and serve.

Helpful hint: Keep brown sugar in an airtight jar or tin and it will stay spoonably soft. You can also tuck a piece of fresh bread into the container to help keep the sugar moist.

FAT: 3G/12%
CALORIES: 234
SATURATED FAT: .5G
CARBOHYDRATE: 21G
PROTEIN: 30G
CHOLESTEROL: 44MG
SODIUM: 366MG

GRILLED SCALLOPS WITH THAI NOODLE SALAD

SERVES: 4
WORKING TIME: 30 MINUTES
TOTAL TIME: 50 MINUTES

2 teaspoons grated lime zest
¼ cup reduced-sodium soy sauce
1 pound sea scallops
8 ounces linguine
¼ cup fresh lime juice
3 tablespoons honey
1 tablespoon dark Oriental sesame oil
½ teaspoon anchovy paste
¼ teaspoon hot pepper sauce
¼ cup chopped fresh cilantro or parsley
2 tablespoons chopped fresh basil
½ teaspoon dried mint
1 cup shredded Napa cabbage or green cabbage
1½ cups diced mango
2 carrots, shredded
2 cloves garlic, minced
16 cherry tomatoes

1. In a medium bowl, combine 1 teaspoon of the lime zest, 1 tablespoon of the soy sauce, and the scallops. Set aside to marinate at room temperature while you make the noodle salad and preheat the grill.

2. In a large pot of boiling water, cook the linguine until tender. Drain well and rinse under cold water. Meanwhile, in a large bowl, combine the remaining 1 teaspoon lime zest, remaining 3 tablespoons soy sauce, the lime juice, honey, sesame oil, anchovy paste, and hot pepper sauce. Add the cilantro, basil, mint, cabbage, mango, carrots, and garlic, tossing to coat. Add the drained pasta to the mango-vegetable mixture, tossing gently to combine.

3. Preheat the grill to a medium heat. Thread the tomatoes onto 2 skewers. Thread the scallops onto 2 skewers. Spray the rack—off the grill—with nonstick cooking spray (see page 6). Grill the kebabs, covered, turning once, for 6 minutes or until the tomatoes are just beginning to split. Remove the tomato skewers and continue to cook the scallops for 5 minutes, or until just opaque.

4. Transfer the noodle salad to a serving platter. Surround with the scallops and tomatoes. Drizzle any dressing remaining in the bowl over the scallops and serve.

The Thai word for an elaborately arranged salad such as this is, appropriately, "yum"! The ingredient list for this "yum" may seem unusual, but all the flavors miraculously merge, bound together by the tangy lime dressing. The use of several different herbs—here, cilantro, basil, and mint—is typically Thai.

FAT: 6G/11%
CALORIES: 476
SATURATED FAT: .8G
CARBOHYDRATE: 79G
PROTEIN: 29G
CHOLESTEROL: 38MG
SODIUM: 843MG

JAMAICAN JERKED SHRIMP WITH PINEAPPLE

SERVES: 4
WORKING TIME: 25 MINUTES
TOTAL TIME: 30 MINUTES

The Caribbean spice blend called "jerk" adds an intriguing mixture of hot (cayenne) and sweet (cinnamon and allspice) flavors to barbecued chicken, meat, and seafood. Jerk works deliciously on this shrimp—and a minty pineapple relish is the perfect Caribbean way to cool the fire.

5 scallions, thinly sliced

2 tablespoons minced fresh ginger

3 cloves garlic, minced

2 teaspoons olive oil

½ teaspoon ground allspice

½ teaspoon freshly ground black pepper

¼ teaspoon cinnamon

⅛ teaspoon cayenne pepper

¾ teaspoon salt

1 tablespoon firmly packed dark brown sugar

24 large shrimp (about 1 pound), shelled and deveined

20-ounce can juice-packed pineapple wedges, drained

1 large red bell pepper, diced

2 tablespoons fresh lime juice

2 tablespoons chopped fresh mint

1. In a large bowl, combine 4 of the scallions, 1 tablespoon plus 2 teaspoons of the ginger, the garlic, oil, allspice, black pepper, cinnamon, cayenne, ½ teaspoon of the salt, and 1 teaspoon of the brown sugar. Add the shrimp, tossing well to coat. Set aside to marinate at room temperature while the grill preheats.

2. Preheat the grill with the grill topper to a medium heat. (When ready to cook, spray the grill topper—off the grill—with nonstick cooking spray; see page 6.)

3. Meanwhile, in a medium bowl, combine the pineapple, bell pepper, lime juice, the remaining scallion, remaining 1 teaspoon ginger, remaining ¼ teaspoon salt, and remaining 2 teaspoons brown sugar. Stir in the mint and set aside.

4. Place the shrimp on the grill topper and grill, covered, turning once, for 4 minutes or until just opaque. Divide the shrimp among 4 plates and serve with the pineapple mixture on the side.

Helpful hint: You can marinate the shrimp for up to 12 hours in the refrigerator.

FAT: 4G/15%
CALORIES: 240
SATURATED FAT: .6G
CARBOHYDRATE: 32G
PROTEIN: 20G
CHOLESTEROL: 140MG
SODIUM: 555MG

SERVES: 4
WORKING TIME: 15 MINUTES
TOTAL TIME: 20 MINUTES

Halibut
*is great for grilling,
and our tomato-basil
sauce, along with green
beans and a salad
make this a quick and
delicious meal.*

½ cup orange juice

⅓ cup dry white wine

1 clove garlic, crushed and peeled

¼ teaspoon red pepper flakes

4 halibut steaks (about 1½ pounds total)

1 tomato, diced

2 scallions, thinly sliced

¼ cup chopped fresh parsley

¼ cup chopped fresh basil

1 teaspoon olive oil

½ teaspoon salt

1. In a nonaluminum pan, combine ¼ cup of the orange juice, the wine, garlic, and red pepper flakes. Add the halibut, turning to coat. Set aside to marinate at room temperature while you make the tomato-herb sauce and preheat the grill.

2. In a medium bowl, combine the tomato, scallions, parsley, basil, oil, salt, and the remaining ¼ cup orange juice.

3. Preheat the grill to a medium heat. Spray the rack—off the grill—with nonstick cooking spray (see page 6). Grill the halibut, covered, turning once, for 6 minutes or until the halibut is just opaque. Place the halibut on 4 plates, top with the tomato-herb sauce, and serve.

Helpful hint: You can marinate the halibut for up to 4 hours in the refrigerator. Bring the fish to room temperature before grilling.

FAT: 5G/22%
CALORIES: 204
SATURATED FAT: .6G
CARBOHYDRATE: 7G
PROTEIN: 30G
CHOLESTEROL: 44MG
SODIUM: 355MG

HERBED FLOUNDER ROLLS

Serves: 4
Working time: 15 minutes
Total time: 25 minutes

¼ cup plain nonfat yogurt

1 tablespoon reduced-fat mayonnaise

1 red bell pepper, finely diced

3 tablespoons chopped fresh parsley

1 teaspoon dried tarragon

¾ teaspoon grated lemon zest

Four 6-ounce flounder fillets, any visible bones removed

2 tablespoons fresh lemon juice

½ teaspoon salt

¼ teaspoon freshly ground black pepper

3 tablespoons plain dried bread crumbs

1. In a small bowl, combine the yogurt, mayonnaise, bell pepper, 1 tablespoon of the parsley, ¼ teaspoon of the tarragon, and ¼ teaspoon of the lemon zest. Cover and refrigerate until serving time.

2. Preheat the grill with the grill topper to a medium heat. (When ready to cook, spray the grill topper—off the grill—with non-stick cooking spray; see page 6.)

3. Lay the flounder fillets flat, skinned-side up. Season with the lemon juice, salt, and black pepper. In a small bowl, combine the bread crumbs, the remaining 2 tablespoons parsley, remaining ¾ teaspoon tarragon, and remaining ½ teaspoon lemon zest. Sprinkle the mixture over the flounder, and starting from a short side, neatly roll up each fillet.

4. Grill the flounder rolls on the grill topper, seam-side down, covered, turning once, for 5 minutes or until the fish is just opaque in the center of the roll. Place the rolls on 4 plates, top with the bell pepper-tartar sauce, and serve.

Helpful hint: For a more traditional flavor, add 2 teaspoons of minced dill pickle to the tartar sauce.

Fat: 3g/13%
Calories: 204
Saturated Fat: .7g
Carbohydrate: 8g
Protein: 34g
Cholesterol: 82mg
Sodium: 497mg

A flavor-packed tartar sauce tops these lemon-herb seasoned flounder rolls. Asparagus is the perfect accompaniment.

Mixed Seafood Kebabs with Parslied Pasta

Serves: 4
Working time: 25 minutes
Total time: 35 minutes

These festive kebabs, generously appointed with fresh seafood, could bear the French name for skewered food, brochettes. Shrimp, scallops, and big chunks of swordfish are the party-perfect elements of these kebabs, which are basted with a seasoned roasted-red-pepper purée. The grilled seafood is served on a bed of parslied pasta.

8 ounces orzo or other small pasta shape
½ cup chopped fresh parsley
2 teaspoons grated lemon zest
¾ teaspoon salt
12-ounce jar roasted red peppers, rinsed and drained
2 scallions, cut into large pieces
2 tablespoons no-salt-added tomato paste
½ teaspoon Worcestershire sauce
1 teaspoon ground cumin
1 teaspoon ground coriander
¼ teaspoon dried tarragon
¼ teaspoon freshly ground black pepper
½ pound shrimp, shelled and deveined
½ pound sea scallops
½ pound swordfish, cut into ¾-inch cubes

1. In a large pot of boiling water, cook the orzo until just tender. Drain well and transfer to a medium bowl. Add the parsley, 1 teaspoon of the lemon zest, and ¼ teaspoon of the salt. Cover loosely to keep warm.

2. Preheat the grill to a medium heat. (When ready to cook, spray the rack—off the grill—with nonstick cooking spray; see page 6.)

3. In a blender or food processor, combine the roasted red peppers, scallions, tomato paste, Worcestershire sauce, cumin, coriander, tarragon, black pepper, the remaining 1 teaspoon lemon zest, and remaining ½ teaspoon salt. Purée until smooth.

4. Alternately thread the shrimp, scallops, and swordfish onto 4 skewers. Brush the red pepper mixture onto the kebabs and grill, covered, turning occasionally and basting with the remaining red pepper mixture, for 6 to 8 minutes or until the seafood is just opaque. Divide the pasta among 4 plates, top with the kebabs, and serve with any remaining red pepper sauce.

Helpful hint: When buying seafood, be sure that it smells slightly sweet, and not at all "fishy." If the scallops are in a package, there should be only a small amount of liquid surrounding them.

Fat: 5g/11%
Calories: 417
Saturated Fat: 1g
Carbohydrate: 52g
Protein: 38g
Cholesterol: 112mg
Sodium: 780mg

GRILLED TUNA SALAD NIÇOISE

SERVES: 4
WORKING TIME: 25 MINUTES
TOTAL TIME: 35 MINUTES PLUS MARINATING TIME

2 tablespoons fresh lemon juice

1 tablespoon drained white horseradish

1 clove garlic, minced

1 pound tuna steak

1½ pounds small red potatoes, cut into ¾-inch cubes

1 pound green beans

7 oil-cured black olives, pitted

2 tablespoons red wine vinegar

1½ tablespoons olive oil

1 tablespoon Dijon mustard

¼ teaspoon salt

¼ teaspoon freshly ground black pepper

8 leaves of Boston lettuce

1 pound plum tomatoes, cut into wedges

1. In a nonaluminum pan, combine 1 tablespoon of the lemon juice, the horseradish, and garlic. Add the tuna, turning to coat. Set aside to marinate at room temperature for 30 minutes or up to 4 hours in the refrigerator.

2. In a large pot of boiling water, cook the potatoes for 5 minutes. Add the green beans and cook until the potatoes are firm-tender, about 10 minutes. Drain the potatoes and green beans and rinse under cold water.

3. Meanwhile, in a blender or food processor, combine 3 of the olives, 2 tablespoons of water, the vinegar, oil, mustard, salt, pepper, and the remaining 1 tablespoon lemon juice and process until smooth. Set the dressing aside.

4. Preheat the grill to a medium heat. Spray the rack—off the grill— with nonstick cooking spray (see page 6). Grill the tuna, covered, for 6 to 8 minutes, or just until firm to the touch. Let stand for 10 minutes before slicing. Line 4 plates with the lettuce leaves and arrange the potatoes, green beans, tomatoes, and tuna slices on top. Chop the remaining 4 olives and sprinkle them over the plates. Drizzle with the dressing and serve.

Helpful hint: Horseradish loses its flavor over time. If you've had a jar of horseradish in the refrigerator for longer than a year, replace it.

FAT: 12G/26%
CALORIES: 413
SATURATED FAT: 2.2G
CARBOHYDRATE: 46G
PROTEIN: 30G
CHOLESTEROL: 38MG
SODIUM: 438MG

Even in its native land— the south of France— salade Niçoise is usually made with canned tuna. In our version, slices of grilled tuna steak join the traditional red potatoes, green beans, tomatoes, and olives in a mustard vinaigrette for a more subtle flavor. While olives are high in fat, the intense flavor of just a few goes a long way. Serve with crusty bread.

GRILLED SHRIMP AND ASPARAGUS SALAD

SERVES: 4
WORKING TIME: 30 MINUTES
TOTAL TIME: 45 MINUTES

This truly luxurious main course offers great flexibility for entertaining. It can be served when the shrimp are still hot from the grill, slightly cooled, or even chilled—whatever suits your schedule. Although this salad can be made anytime of year, it's especially good in the spring when tender young asparagus is widely available.

2 tablespoons fresh lemon juice
2 teaspoons Dijon mustard
1½ teaspoons olive oil
¼ teaspoon salt
¼ cup chopped fresh parsley
1 teaspoon grated lemon zest
1 clove garlic, minced
1 pound large shrimp, shelled and deveined
1 pound asparagus, tough ends trimmed, cut diagonally into 2-inch lengths
½ cup finely diced red bell pepper
1 tablespoon finely chopped pecans

1. In a medium bowl, combine the lemon juice, mustard, oil, and salt. Set the dressing aside. In another medium bowl, combine the parsley, lemon zest, and garlic. Add the shrimp, tossing to coat. Set aside to marinate while the grill preheats.

2. Preheat the grill with the grill topper to a medium heat. (When ready to cook the shrimp, spray the grill topper—off the grill—with nonstick cooking spray; see page 6.)

3. Tear off a 24-inch length of heavy-duty foil and fold in half to form a 12 x 18-inch rectangle. Place the asparagus and 2 table-spoons of water in the center of the rectangle and seal the packet (see page 8). Place the packet on the grill rack and cook for 10 minutes or until the asparagus is crisp-tender. Add the asparagus to the dressing.

4. Grill the shrimp on the grill topper, turning once, for 3 to 4 minutes or until the shrimp are just opaque. Add the cooked shrimp to the asparagus, tossing to coat thoroughly. Transfer the mixture to a platter, sprinkle with the bell pepper and pecans, and serve warm, at room temperature, or chilled.

Helpful hint: If you are serving the salad chilled, you can prepare it up to 8 hours in advance.

FAT: 5G/29%
CALORIES: 156
SATURATED FAT: 0.7G
CARBOHYDRATE: 7G
PROTEIN: 22G
CHOLESTEROL: 140MG
SODIUM: 335MG

Striped Bass with Green Curry Sauce

SERVES: 4
WORKING TIME: 15 MINUTES
TOTAL TIME: 25 MINUTES

Indian food is not the only cuisine that takes advantage of curry. Thai curries—like this one—are blended from ingredients such as fresh chilies, scallions, cilantro, lime juice, and a range of spices from sweet to hot; coconut cream stirred into curry sauces serves to tame the fire. Here, flaked coconut adds flavor but little fat to this lively sauce. Serve with a salad.

½ cup packed fresh cilantro or parsley leaves

2 scallions, cut into large pieces

2 tablespoons fresh lime juice

3 tablespoons flaked coconut

1 jalapeño pepper, seeded and sliced

1½ teaspoons ground cumin

¾ teaspoon salt

½ teaspoon freshly ground black pepper

1 cup long-grain rice

1 teaspoon turmeric

4 striped bass fillets, skin on, any visible bones removed (about 1½ pounds total)

1. In a food processor or blender, combine the cilantro, scallions, lime juice, coconut, jalapeño, cumin, ½ teaspoon of the salt, and the black pepper. Add ¼ cup of water and process until the green curry paste is smooth and well combined, about 30 seconds.

2. In a medium saucepan, combine the rice, 2 tablespoons of the green curry paste, 2½ cups of water, the turmeric, and the remaining ¼ teaspoon salt. Bring to a boil, reduce to a simmer, cover, and cook until the rice is tender, about 17 minutes.

3. Preheat the grill to a medium heat. Spread the remaining green curry paste on the skinless side of the fish. Spray the rack—off the grill—with nonstick cooking spray (see page 6). Grill the fish, skin-side down, for 5 minutes or until the fish is just opaque. Divide the fish and rice among 4 plates and serve.

Helpful hint: In place of the striped bass, you can substitute another lean, flavorful fish, such as sea bass, red snapper, or tilefish.

FAT: 5G/13%
CALORIES: 355
SATURATED FAT: 1.9G
CARBOHYDRATE: 41G
PROTEIN: 33G
CHOLESTEROL: 130MG
SODIUM: 540MG

Barbecued Salmon with Plum Sauce

Serves: 4
Working time: 25 minutes
Total time: 40 minutes

*A*n *herbed white-bean salad is the easy make-ahead side dish for this marinated and grilled salmon.*

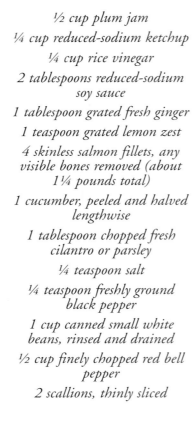

½ cup plum jam

¼ cup reduced-sodium ketchup

¼ cup rice vinegar

2 tablespoons reduced-sodium soy sauce

1 tablespoon grated fresh ginger

1 teaspoon grated lemon zest

4 skinless salmon fillets, any visible bones removed (about 1¼ pounds total)

1 cucumber, peeled and halved lengthwise

1 tablespoon chopped fresh cilantro or parsley

¼ teaspoon salt

¼ teaspoon freshly ground black pepper

1 cup canned small white beans, rinsed and drained

½ cup finely chopped red bell pepper

2 scallions, thinly sliced

1. In a small bowl, combine the jam, ketchup, 1 tablespoon of the vinegar, the soy sauce, ginger, and lemon zest. Measure out ¼ cup of the plum sauce to use as a baste. Set the remaining plum sauce aside. Brush the salmon lightly with 2 tablespoons of the baste and set aside to marinate while the grill preheats.

2. With a spoon, scoop out the seeds from each cucumber half and finely chop the halves. In a medium bowl, combine the remaining 3 tablespoons vinegar, the cilantro, salt, and black pepper. Add the cucumber, white beans, bell pepper, and scallions, tossing to coat.

3. Preheat the grill with the grill topper to a medium heat. Spray the grill topper—off the grill—with nonstick cooking spray (see page 6). Grill the salmon on the grill topper, turning once and brushing with the remaining baste, for 14 minutes or until just opaque. Place the salmon and bean salad on 4 plates and serve with the remaining plum sauce on the side.

Helpful hints: You can marinate the salmon for up to 2 hours in the refrigerator. The bean salad can be made 1 day ahead and refrigerated.

FAT: 10G/24%
CALORIES: 375
SATURATED FAT: 1.4G
CARBOHYDRATE: 40G
PROTEIN: 33G
CHOLESTEROL: 78MG
SODIUM: 756MG

GINGER-SOY SWORDFISH

SERVES: 4
WORKING TIME: 35 MINUTES
TOTAL TIME: 35 MINUTES PLUS MARINATING TIME

¼ cup plus 2 tablespoons orange marmalade

3 tablespoons reduced-sodium soy sauce

1 tablespoon dry sherry or apple juice

1 tablespoon grated fresh ginger

1 tablespoon balsamic vinegar

1 tablespoon dark Oriental sesame oil

1 clove garlic, minced

¼ teaspoon freshly ground black pepper

1¼ pounds swordfish steak, cut into 4 serving pieces

1 cup basmati rice

1 carrot, shredded

2 tablespoons rice vinegar

2 teaspoons honey

¼ cup chopped fresh parsley

1. In a nonaluminum pan, combine ¼ cup of the marmalade, 2 tablespoons of the soy sauce, the sherry, 1 teaspoon of the ginger, the balsamic vinegar, sesame oil, garlic, and pepper. Measure out 3 tablespoons of the ginger-soy mixture and set aside. Add the swordfish to the mixture remaining in the pan, turning to coat. Set aside to marinate at room temperature for 20 minutes or up to 2 hours in the refrigerator.

2. Meanwhile, in a medium saucepan, bring 2 cups of water to a boil and reduce to a simmer. Add the rice, carrot, rice vinegar, honey, and the remaining 2 tablespoons marmalade, remaining 1 tablespoon soy sauce, and remaining 2 teaspoons ginger and stir to combine. Cover and cook for 10 minutes. Remove the pan from heat, stir in the parsley, and let stand, covered, for 7 minutes.

3. Preheat the grill to a medium heat. Spray the rack—off the grill—with nonstick cooking spray (see page 6). Remove the swordfish from the marinade and grill, covered, turning once and basting with the marinade, for 8 minutes or until just opaque. Place the rice and fish on 4 plates, drizzle the reserved ginger-soy mixture over the fish, and serve.

Helpful hint: Basmati rice, which is of Indian origin, has a wonderfully nutlike fragrance and flavor.

FAT: 9G/18%
CALORIES: 447
SATURATED FAT: 1.9G
CARBOHYDRATE: 63G
PROTEIN: 31G
CHOLESTEROL: 49MG
SODIUM: 609MG

M*eaty swordfish pleases even those who prefer beef to fish. Snow peas and water chestnuts offer a nice textural contrast.*

93

COD AND SUMMER VEGETABLES IN PACKETS

SERVES: 4
WORKING TIME: 25 MINUTES
TOTAL TIME: 50 MINUTES

5½-ounce can spicy tomato-vegetable juice

2 tablespoons dry white wine

4 teaspoons chopped fresh tarragon or basil

1 tablespoon drained white horseradish

2 teaspoons olive oil

½ teaspoon salt

¼ teaspoon freshly ground black pepper

¾ cup bulghur (cracked wheat)

4 cod fillets, any visible bones removed (about 1¼ pounds total)

2 tomatoes, sliced

2 yellow summer squash, cut into 2-inch julienne strips

1 zucchini, cut into 2-inch julienne strips

1. Preheat the grill to a medium heat.

2. In a small bowl, combine the tomato-vegetable juice, wine, tarragon, horseradish, oil, salt, and pepper. Set aside.

3. Tear off four 24-inch lengths of heavy-duty foil, fold each in half to form a 12 x 18-inch rectangle and spray with nonstick cooking spray. Dividing evenly, place the bulghur in the center of each rectangle. Top with the cod, tomato slices, yellow squash, and zucchini. Spoon the tomato sauce on top and seal the packets (see page 8).

4. Grill the packets, covered, for 25 minutes, or until the vegetables are crisp-tender and the fish is just opaque. Place a packet on each of 4 plates and serve.

Helpful hint: You may be doubtful about putting uncooked bulghur in the packet, but when you open the foil you'll see that the grain has absorbed the liquid and become tender and fluffy.

You can't beat a meal cooked in packets for easy post-cooking cleanup: All you need to do is clean the bowl in which you've mixed the sauce and recycle the foil used for the packets. The sealed pouches allow the flavors of the cod, vegetables, bulghur, and seasonings to mingle while they steam over the grill.

FAT: 5G/16%
CALORIES: 285
SATURATED FAT: .6G
CARBOHYDRATE: 30G
PROTEIN: 31G
CHOLESTEROL: 61MG
SODIUM: 487MG

Bluefish possesses a succulent richness and a distinctive flavor. Here, the richness is balanced with a piquant marinade that includes chili sauce, horseradish, and mustard. The potatoes that cook along with the fish are semi-slit and spread—inside and out—with a garlic mixture. Serve with steamed sugar snap peas and carrots.

Barbecued Bluefish with Grilled Potatoes

SERVES: 4
WORKING TIME: 20 MINUTES
TOTAL TIME: 50 MINUTES

¼ cup chili sauce

1 tablespoon plus 1½ teaspoons drained white horseradish

2 teaspoons coarse-grained mustard

¼ cup fresh lemon juice

⅜ teaspoon freshly ground black pepper

4 bluefish fillets, any visible bones removed (about 1 pound total)

3 tablespoons chopped fresh parsley

2 cloves garlic, minced

12 small red potatoes

¼ teaspoon salt

1. In a nonaluminum pan, combine the chili sauce, horseradish, mustard, 2 tablespoons of the lemon juice, and ¼ teaspoon of the pepper. Add the fish, turning to coat. Set aside to marinate while you prepare the potatoes and preheat the grill.

2. Preheat the grill with the grill topper to a medium heat. (When ready to cook, spray the grill topper—off the grill—with nonstick cooking spray; see page 6.)

3. In a small bowl, combine the parsley, garlic, and remaining 2 tablespoons lemon juice. Using a small sharp knife, make slits in the potatoes ⅛ inch apart (see tip; top photo) Brush the potatoes with the lemon-parsley mixture (bottom photo), spreading it in between the slits. Sprinkle the potatoes with the salt and the remaining ⅛ teaspoon pepper. Tear off four 12-inch lengths of heavy-duty foil and wrap 3 potatoes in each piece of foil.

4. Grill the potato packets on the grill rack and the bluefish on the grill topper, covered, turning the fish once and basting it with the marinade, for 10 to 15 minutes or until the fish is just opaque. Remove the fish and cook the potatoes for 10 to 15 minutes, or until firm-tender. Place the fish and potatoes on 4 plates and serve.

Helpful hint: You can marinate the bluefish for up to 2 hours in the refrigerator.

FAT: 5G/16%
CALORIES: 287
SATURATED FAT: 1G
CARBOHYDRATE: 32G
PROTEIN: 26G
CHOLESTEROL: 67MG
SODIUM: 479MG

TIP

To make the slits, slice almost all the way through each potato, leaving the potato intact. Brush the lemon-parsley mixture into the slits and then around the outside of the potato to infuse it with flavor.

SALMON STEAKS WITH PESTO AND PEPPERS

SERVES: 4
WORKING TIME: 40 MINUTES
TOTAL TIME: 55 MINUTES

Two of late summer's most glorious offerings—bush-sized bunches of basil and a rainbow of bell peppers—come together in this extraordinary one-dish dinner. This slimmed-down pesto is made with the smallest possible quantity of oil, and the high-fat nuts are omitted altogether. Still, its intense flavor infuses both the salmon and the vegetables.

1 cup reduced-sodium chicken broth, defatted

5 cloves garlic, peeled

2 teaspoons olive oil

2 cups packed fresh basil leaves

2 tablespoons grated Parmesan cheese

2 tablespoons plain dried bread crumbs

1 tablespoon fresh lemon juice, plus 1 lemon, cut into wedges

½ teaspoon salt

¼ teaspoon freshly ground black pepper

2 cups frozen corn kernels, thawed

4 scallions, sliced

4 bell peppers, mixed colors, halved lengthwise and seeded, stems left on

4 salmon steaks (1 pound total)

1. In a medium saucepan, combine the broth, garlic, and oil. Bring to a boil over medium-high heat and cook until reduced to about ¼ cup, 12 to 15 minutes. Let cool slightly and place in a blender or food processor along with the basil, Parmesan, bread crumbs, lemon juice, salt, and black pepper and process until the pesto is smooth. In a medium bowl, combine the corn, scallions, and half of the pesto, tossing to combine.

2. Preheat the grill to a medium heat. Spray the rack—off the grill—with nonstick cooking spray (see page 6). Grill the pepper halves, cut-sides down, for 8 minutes. Invert them and spoon the corn mixture into them, dividing evenly. Place the peppers toward the outer edges of the grill to cook while you grill the salmon.

3. Brush the salmon steaks lightly with some of the remaining pesto and place them on the grill. Grill the salmon, covered, turning once and basting liberally with the remaining pesto, for 12 minutes or until just opaque. Place the salmon and peppers on 4 plates and serve with lemon wedges. Remove the salmon skin before eating.

Helpful hint: An equally delicious pesto with a Mexican flavor can be made with fresh cilantro instead of basil.

FAT: 11G/29%
CALORIES: 334
SATURATED FAT: 1.9G
CARBOHYDRATE: 38G
PROTEIN: 28G
CHOLESTEROL: 57MG
SODIUM: 567MG

SALMON BURGERS

SERVES: 4
WORKING TIME: 15 MINUTES
TOTAL TIME: 35 MINUTES

Partner these patties with a yogurt-dressed potato salad and crisp lettuce; tuck the greens into the bun if you like.

1 large baking potato (10 ounces), peeled and thinly sliced

15-ounce can pink salmon, drained and flaked

¼ cup chopped fresh parsley

2 tablespoons reduced-fat mayonnaise

2 tablespoons plain dried bread crumbs

2 scallions, thinly sliced

2 tablespoons fresh lemon juice

1 teaspoon dried tarragon

½ teaspoon salt

½ teaspoon hot pepper sauce

1 small red bell pepper, finely diced

4 hamburger rolls

4 tomato slices

1. In a large pot of boiling water, cook the potato until tender, about 15 minutes. Drain well and mash.

2. Preheat the grill with the grill topper to a medium heat. (When ready to cook, spray the grill topper—off the grill—with non-stick cooking spray; see page 6.)

3. In a large bowl, combine the salmon, parsley, mayonnaise, bread crumbs, scallions, lemon juice, tarragon, salt, hot pepper sauce, and mashed potato, stirring to mix. Fold in the bell pepper and mix again. Shape into four 1-inch-thick patties.

4. Place the burgers on the grill topper and grill, covered, turning them once, for 8 minutes or until warmed through and lightly browned. Grill the buns, cut-sides down, for 30 seconds to lightly toast. Divide the buns among 4 plates, top with the salmon patties and tomato slices, and serve.

Helpful hint: For light, juicy salmon burgers, handle the salmon mixture lightly. If you compress it too much, the burgers may be dense and dry.

FAT: 9G/24%
CALORIES: 337
SATURATED FAT: 2.1G
CARBOHYDRATE: 38G
PROTEIN: 25G
CHOLESTEROL: 34MG
SODIUM: 920MG

VEGETABLES

4

MIXED VEGETABLE PACKETS

SERVES: 4
WORKING TIME: 20 MINUTES
TOTAL TIME: 45 MINUTES

The combination of potatoes, chick-peas, summery vegetables, fresh herbs, and cheese makes for a truly substantial meal here. You may want to add some pencil-thin Italian bread sticks for crisp contrast. Remember, when topping a dish with cheese, the more finely you grate it, the further it goes: Less cheese means less fat.

1¼ pounds small red potatoes, thinly sliced

1½ tablespoons chopped fresh tarragon or 1½ teaspoons dried

2 shallots or scallions, finely chopped

½ teaspoon salt

¼ teaspoon freshly ground black pepper

1 cup canned chick-peas, rinsed and drained

2 zucchini, thinly sliced on the diagonal

8 plum tomatoes, quartered lengthwise

¾ cup shredded Gruyère or Swiss cheese (3 ounces)

¼ cup dry white wine

1. Preheat the grill to a medium heat. Tear off four 24-inch lengths of heavy-duty foil, fold each in half to form a 12 x 18-inch rectangle, and spray with nonstick cooking spray.

2. In a small bowl, toss together the potatoes, tarragon, shallots, salt, pepper, and chick-peas. Dividing evenly, spoon the mixture into the center of each of the four rectangles of foil. Arrange the zucchini and tomatoes on top of the potato mixture, sprinkle with the cheese, and spoon 1 tablespoon of wine into each packet.

3. Seal the packets (see page 8) and grill, covered, for 20 to 25 minutes or until the potatoes are tender. Place the packets on 4 plates and serve.

Helpful hint: You can prepare the vegetable packets up to 8 hours in advance and keep them refrigerated until you are ready to grill.

FAT: 10G/29%
CALORIES: 303
SATURATED FAT: 4.1G
CARBOHYDRATE: 40G
PROTEIN: 14G
CHOLESTEROL: 23MG
SODIUM: 448MG

Some vegetarians feel neglected at barbecues, where meat is often the main attraction. But these fresh-from-the-grill burritos are a sure crowd-pleaser. The tortillas are loaded with a satisfying two-bean filling and melted Monterey jack cheese. Shredded lettuce, tomatoes, and avocados form the Mexican-style side salad.

Vegetable Burritos

SERVES: 4
WORKING TIME: 30 MINUTES
TOTAL TIME: 45 MINUTES

½ teaspoon olive oil

1 red bell pepper, cut into thin strips

1 zucchini, cut into 2-inch julienne strips

2 cloves garlic, minced

4 scallions, sliced

1 tablespoon chili powder

1 teaspoon ground cumin

4½-ounce can chopped mild green chilies, drained

15-ounce can red kidney beans, rinsed and drained

14½-ounce can no-salt-added stewed tomatoes, drained and finely chopped

15-ounce can black beans, rinsed and drained

Four 8-inch flour tortillas

½ cup shredded Monterey jack or Cheddar cheese (2 ounces)

1. In large nonstick skillet, heat the oil until hot but not smoking over medium heat. Add the bell pepper and zucchini and cook until the bell pepper is softened, about 5 minutes. Stir in the garlic, scallions, chili powder, and cumin. Cook for 2 minutes to soften the scallions and blend the flavors. Add the green chilies, kidney beans, and tomatoes. Cook for 3 minutes, mashing about half of the beans to thicken. Add the black beans, stirring to combine.

2. Preheat the grill to a medium heat. Tear off four 24-inch lengths of heavy-duty foil, fold each in half to form a 12 x 18-inch rectangle, and spray with nonstick cooking spray.

3. Place a tortilla in the center of each rectangle. Spoon the bean mixture into the center of each tortilla, spreading it into a rectangle. Top with the cheese. Fold the tortilla over the filling and roll up (see tip). Seal the packets (see page 8) and grill for 12 minutes, or until warmed through. Place the tortillas on 4 plates, cut each tortilla in half, and serve.

Helpful hint: The bean mixture can be prepared up to 12 hours in advance, but don't assemble the burritos more than 1 hour ahead of time or the tortillas will get mushy.

FAT: 10G/24%
CALORIES: 373
SATURATED FAT: 3.1G
CARBOHYDRATE: 55G
PROTEIN: 19G
CHOLESTEROL: 15MG
SODIUM: 784MG

TIP

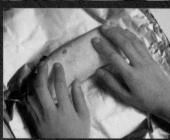

Fold two sides of the tortilla over the filling. Fold up the bottom edge of the tortilla and carefully roll the burrito into a neat bundle, ending seam-side down.

GRILLED PIZZA

SERVES: 4
WORKING TIME: 20 MINUTES
TOTAL TIME: 30 MINUTES

8-ounce can no-salt-added tomato sauce

1 teaspoon dried basil

½ teaspoon dried oregano

¼ teaspoon hot pepper sauce

1 zucchini, shredded

½ teaspoon salt

1 pound store-bought pizza dough

1 cup shredded part-skim mozzarella cheese (4 ounces)

1 cup frozen corn kernels, thawed

4 scallions, sliced

1. In a small bowl, combine the tomato sauce, basil, oregano, and hot pepper sauce. Set aside. In another small bowl, combine the zucchini and salt and let stand for 10 minutes. With your hands, squeeze the zucchini dry and set it aside.

2. Meanwhile, preheat the grill to a medium heat. (When ready to cook, spray the rack—off the grill—with nonstick cooking spray; see page 6.)

3. Roll the dough out on a floured surface to an 11-inch circle. Place the dough on an inverted baking sheet sprinkled with flour. Slide the dough onto the grill rack and grill for 2 to 3 minutes, or until lightly browned on the bottom. Using two spatulas, flip the dough. Spread the reserved tomato sauce evenly over the dough. Sprinkle the zucchini, mozzarella, corn, and scallions on top and grill, covered, for 3 to 4 minutes or until the cheese is bubbly. Let stand for 5 minutes before slicing.

Helpful hints: You can buy ready-to-use pizza dough from many pizzerias and Italian specialty stores; you may also find it in the dairy case in the supermarket. Or, you can use the refrigerated dough that comes in a roll: This type of dough can simply be patted out into a rectangle, just as it comes from the package, rather than rolled into a circle.

FAT: 9G/18%
CALORIES: 443
SATURATED FAT: 3.7G
CARBOHYDRATE: 72G
PROTEIN: 20G
CHOLESTEROL: 16MG
SODIUM: 919MG

Cooking pizza on the grill gives it some of the tantalizing smokiness of pizza baked in a wood-fired or brick pizza oven. Feel free to experiment with other vegetable toppings, such as mushrooms, sliced onions, or roasted bell peppers— just grill them (on a grill topper coated with nonstick cooking spray) before browning the pizza dough.

GRILLED EGGPLANT AND FETA WITH PASTA

SERVES: 4
WORKING TIME: 25 MINUTES
TOTAL TIME: 35 MINUTES

Candlelight and an evening breeze (and perhaps a glass of chilled white wine and a crisp green salad) are all you need to make this meal complete. The combination of eggplant, feta, and mint is quintessentially Greek; the roasted vegetables and cheese virtually melt into a rich-tasting sauce. Vary the dish with other pasta shapes, such as ziti or radiatore.

8 ounces medium pasta shells

1 pound plum tomatoes, coarsely chopped

⅓ cup chopped fresh mint

½ cup crumbled feta cheese (2 ounces)

2 teaspoons olive oil

1 teaspoon salt

¼ cup balsamic vinegar

2 teaspoons firmly packed light brown sugar

1 pound eggplant, peeled and cut lengthwise into ½-inch-thick slices

1 zucchini, cut lengthwise into ½-inch-thick slices

1 red bell pepper, halved lengthwise and seeded

1. Preheat the grill with the grill topper to a medium heat. In a large pot of boiling water, cook the pasta until tender. Drain. In a large bowl, combine the tomatoes, mint, feta, oil, and salt. Add the drained pasta, tossing to coat.

2. In a small bowl, combine the vinegar and brown sugar. Spray the grill topper—off the grill—with nonstick cooking spray (see page 6). Brush the eggplant and the zucchini with half of the vinegar mixture. Place the eggplant, zucchini, and bell pepper halves, cut-sides up, on the grill topper and grill, covered, turning once, for 10 minutes or until the eggplant and zucchini are tender and the bell pepper skin is blackened.

3. Cut the eggplant and zucchini into 1-inch pieces and toss with the pasta. Peel the pepper, cut it into large squares, and toss with the pasta along with the remaining vinegar mixture. Divide the mixture among 4 plates and serve at room temperature.

Helpful hint: Double the recipe (except for the pasta) so you can enjoy grilled vegetable sandwiches (on foccacia or semolina bread) the next day.

FAT: 7G/18%
CALORIES: 342
SATURATED FAT: 2.6G
CARBOHYDRATE: 60G
PROTEIN: 12G
CHOLESTEROL: 13MG
SODIUM: 730MG

New Potato and Pepper Salad

Serves: 4
Working time: 20 minutes
Total time: 40 minutes

The popular barbecue side dish, potato salad, takes center stage here, enhanced by the addition of bell peppers, kidney beans, and cheese. Thin-skinned new potatoes are best for skin-on potato salads; red potatoes are prettiest, but tan- or golden-skinned varieties would be equally delicious.

2 pounds small red potatoes
½ cup dry white wine
3 tablespoons distilled white vinegar
2 tablespoons coarse-grained mustard
1 tablespoon capers, rinsed and drained
¼ teaspoon salt
1 red bell pepper, halved lengthwise and seeded
1 green bell pepper, halved lengthwise and seeded
1 small red onion, finely chopped
1 cup diced celery
15-ounce can kidney beans, rinsed and drained
¾ cup crumbled feta or goat cheese (3 ounces)

1. Preheat the grill with the grill topper to a medium heat. (When ready to cook, spray the grill topper—off the grill—with nonstick cooking spray; see page 6.)

2. In a large pot of boiling water, cook the potatoes until firm-tender, about 12 minutes. Drain.

3. Meanwhile in a large bowl, whisk together the wine, vinegar, and mustard. Stir in the capers and salt and set the dressing aside.

4. Grill the potatoes and bell pepper halves, cut-sides down, on the grill topper, covered, for 10 minutes or until the peppers are tender and the potatoes are cooked through. Cut the peppers into large squares, and add to the bowl of dressing. Quarter the potatoes and add to the bowl along with the onion and celery. Fold in the beans and feta and serve warm, at room temperature, or chilled.

Helpful hint: Although this salad tastes wonderful freshly made and warm, you can also make it up to 4 hours ahead of time—the potatoes and peppers will absorb the dressing upon standing for heightened flavor.

Fat: 6g/15%
Calories: 372
Saturated Fat: 3.2g
Carbohydrate: 60g
Protein: 14g
Cholesterol: 19mg
Sodium: 698mg

GRILLED VEGETABLE AND MOZZARELLA SANDWICHES

SERVES: 4
WORKING TIME: 20 MINUTES
TOTAL TIME: 30 MINUTES

2 cups no-salt-added tomato sauce

¼ cup balsamic vinegar

1 teaspoon reduced-sodium soy sauce

½ teaspoon firmly packed light brown sugar

2 large zucchini, cut lengthwise into ¼-inch-thick slices

1 large red onion, thickly sliced

8 slices (½ inch thick) Italian country or peasant bread

3 cloves garlic, peeled and halved

1 cup shredded part-skim mozzarella cheese (4 ounces)

1. Preheat the grill with the grill topper to a medium heat. In a large bowl, combine the tomato sauce, vinegar, soy sauce, and brown sugar. Add the zucchini and onion, tossing to coat. Spray the grill topper—off the grill—with nonstick cooking spray (see page 6). Grill the vegetables on the grill topper, covered, turning occasionally, for 10 minutes or until crisp-tender. Transfer the vegetables to a plate.

2. Rub the bread on both sides with the cut garlic cloves. Grill the bread on one side for 30 seconds to lightly toast. Remove the bread from the grill. Dividing evenly, top the toasted side of the bread with the cheese and grilled vegetables. Return to the grill, and grill, covered, for 30 seconds to toast the second side of the bread and melt the cheese. Place the sandwiches on 4 plates and serve.

Helpful hint: If you have a small grill topper, you may have to grill the vegetables in batches.

FAT: 7G/23%
CALORIES: 269
SATURATED FAT: 3.2G
CARBOHYDRATE: 40G
PROTEIN: 14G
CHOLESTEROL: 16MG
SODIUM: 451MG

These glorious open-face sandwiches—slabs of garlic-rubbed peasant bread topped with grilled zucchini, onions, and melted mozzarella—are the stars of any barbecue. A cool salad of Bibb lettuce, cherry tomatoes, and bell peppers makes a lovely accompaniment.

GRILLED STUFFED MUSHROOMS

SERVES: 4
WORKING TIME: 20 MINUTES
TOTAL TIME: 25 MINUTES PLUS MARINATING TIME

Whether offered as an appetizer or nestled alongside a steak, these garlicky mushroom caps make any meal special.

1 cup reduced-sodium chicken broth, defatted

3 tablespoons Dijon mustard

2 tablespoons fresh lemon juice

½ teaspoon Worcestershire sauce

12 large mushrooms, stems removed and reserved

4 ounces Italian or French bread, crumbled

½ cup chopped fresh parsley

4 scallions, thinly sliced

2 cloves garlic, minced

½ teaspoon salt

1 teaspoon olive oil

1. In a large bowl, combine the broth, mustard, lemon juice, and Worcestershire sauce. Add the mushroom caps, tossing to coat. Set aside to marinate at room temperature for 30 minutes. Reserving the marinade, drain the mushroom caps.

2. Meanwhile, preheat the grill with the grill topper to a medium heat. (When ready to cook, spray the grill topper—off the grill—with nonstick cooking spray; see page 6.)

3. Coarsely chop the mushroom stems and place them in a large bowl. Add the bread, parsley, scallions, garlic, salt, and oil. Add the reserved marinade to the bread mixture, stirring to thoroughly moisten.

4. Grill the mushrooms, stemmed-sides down, on the grill topper, for 5 minutes or until lightly browned. Remove the mushrooms to a work surface, turn them stemmed-sides up, and spoon the stuffing mixture into them. Return to the grill topper and grill, covered, stuffed-sides up, for 4 minutes or until the mushroom caps are tender and the stuffing is piping hot.

Helpful hint: To make these ahead, grill the mushrooms for 5 minutes as directed in step 4, and then stuff them up to 8 hours in advance. Place the stuffed mushrooms in a shallow pan and cover with plastic wrap until you're ready to grill them.

FAT: 3G/19%
CALORIES: 139
SATURATED FAT: .4G
CARBOHYDRATE: 22G
PROTEIN: 6G
CHOLESTEROL: 0MG
SODIUM: 886MG

GRILLED EGGPLANT "CAVIAR"

SERVES: 4
WORKING TIME: 25 MINUTES
TOTAL TIME: 45 MINUTES

2 eggplants (1 pound each)

3 cloves garlic, slivered

¼ cup reduced-sodium chicken broth, defatted

1 green bell pepper, halved lengthwise and seeded

3 yellow or red bell peppers, 1 halved lengthwise and seeded, and 2 cut into wide strips

4 ounces Italian bread, sliced ½ inch thick

2 tablespoons fresh lemon juice

2 tablespoons chopped fresh mint

2 tablespoons chopped fresh parsley

½ teaspoon salt

2 ribs celery, cut into 3-inch sticks

2 carrots, cut into 3-inch sticks

1. Preheat the grill to a medium heat. (When ready to cook, spray the rack—off the grill—with nonstick cooking spray; see page 6.)

2. With a paring knife, make several deep slashes in each eggplant. Push the slivered garlic into the slashes and brush the eggplants with the broth. Grill the eggplants and bell pepper halves, cut-sides up, covered, turning occasionally, for 10 minutes, or until the pepper skin is blackened. Remove the peppers and cook the eggplants for 10 minutes longer or until blackened on all sides. Grill the bread slices for 30 seconds to lightly toast. Set aside.

3. When cool enough to handle, with your fingers, peel the peppers and eggplants and transfer them to a food processor. Add the lemon juice, mint, parsley, and salt and process with on/off pulses until the mixture is not quite smooth and still has some texture. Transfer the "caviar" to a serving bowl and serve with the toast, celery, carrots, and bell pepper strips.

Helpful hint: Lightly grilled pita triangles can be used in place of the Italian bread. You could also carry out the "caviar" theme by accompanying the dip with crustless white-toast points.

FAT: 1G/5%
CALORIES: 171
SATURATED FAT: .3G
CARBOHYDRATE: 36G
PROTEIN: 6G
CHOLESTEROL: 0MG
SODIUM: 519MG

This dark, smoky dip—perfect for parties—will save you a pretty penny over its pricey namesake.

115

Ears of corn come in their own natural package, which also serves as a perfect wrapping for grilling. The husks protect the corn from the heat of the fire while trapping the natural juices (as well as the added seasonings of lime juice and thyme). The small amount of olive oil brushed over the corn is a much healthier option than a slathering of butter.

GRILLED CORN IN THE HUSK

SERVES: 4
WORKING TIME: 15 MINUTES
TOTAL TIME: 35 MINUTES

3 tablespoons fresh lime juice
2 teaspoons olive oil
1 teaspoon dried thyme
4 ears of corn, unhusked
¾ teaspoon salt

1. Preheat the grill to a medium heat. In a small bowl, combine the lime juice, oil, and thyme. Set aside.

2. Peel back the husk from the corn and remove the corn silk, leaving the husk attached (see tip; top photo). Rinse the corn under cold running water to dampen the husks. Brush the lime juice mixture over the corn kernels, then pull the husk back over the corn and tie with kitchen string (bottom photo).

3. Grill the corn, covered, turning as the husks blacken, for 20 minutes or until piping hot. Remove the string and husks, sprinkle the salt over the corn, and serve.

Helpful hint: Try a different herb—such as dried dill, tarragon, oregano, or basil—for a simple variation, or to complement the flavors of the main course.

FAT: 3G/27%
CALORIES: 101
SATURATED FAT: .5G
CARBOHYDRATE: 18G
PROTEIN: 3G
CHOLESTEROL: 0MG
SODIUM: 426MG

TIP

Pull the husk away from the corn, but leave it attached at the base. Carefully remove the silk and discard it. After brushing the corn with the lime juice mixture, bring the husk back up around the ear and tie it at the top and bottom with kitchen string.

VEGETABLE KEBABS

SERVES: 4
WORKING TIME: 25 MINUTES
TOTAL TIME: 40 MINUTES

You don't have to fuss over the main dish when these kebabs are on the menu: They'll elevate the simplest grilled fish or chicken to epicurean heights. (For a completely vegetarian meal, pair the kebabs with a grain or pasta salad.) The summer and winter squashes, bell peppers, and mushrooms are basted with a basil-scented tomato sauce.

1 small butternut squash (1¼ pounds), quartered lengthwise, seeded, and peeled

8-ounce can no-salt-added tomato sauce

2 cloves garlic, minced

2 tablespoons chopped fresh basil

2 teaspoons balsamic vinegar

½ teaspoon ground ginger

¼ teaspoon salt

1 zucchini, cut into 16 rounds

1 yellow or red bell pepper, cut into 16 pieces

16 mushrooms, stems removed

1. Preheat the grill to a medium heat. (When ready to cook, spray the rack—off the grill—with nonstick cooking spray; see page 6.)

2. Cut each of the squash quarters crosswise into 4 large chunks for a total of 16 pieces. In a large pot of boiling water, cook the squash until almost tender, about 4 minutes. Drain. Meanwhile, in a small bowl, combine the tomato sauce, garlic, basil, vinegar, ginger, and salt. Set aside.

3. Alternately thread the squash, zucchini, bell pepper, and mushrooms onto 8 skewers. Brush with some of the tomato mixture. Grill, covered, turning occasionally and basting every 2 minutes with the tomato sauce, for 10 minutes or until the vegetables are tender and richly hued.

Helpful hint: You can make the sauce up to 8 hours in advance and refrigerate it in a covered container until needed.

FAT: 1G/9%
CALORIES: 100
SATURATED FAT: .1G
CARBOHYDRATE: 24G
PROTEIN: 4G
CHOLESTEROL: 0MG
SODIUM: 156MG

GRILLED MUSHROOMS, POTATOES, AND LEEKS

SERVES: 4
WORKING TIME: 15 MINUTES
TOTAL TIME: 30 MINUTES

Try this sesame-fragrant side dish in the fall, when leeks and potatoes are most abundant.

1 pound small red potatoes, halved

3 large leeks

½ cup reduced-sodium chicken broth, defatted

2 tablespoons reduced-sodium soy sauce

2 tablespoons ketchup

2 teaspoons red wine vinegar

1½ teaspoons dark Oriental sesame oil

¼ teaspoon salt

8 large mushrooms, stems removed

½ cup chopped fresh parsley

1. In a large pot of boiling water, cook the potatoes for 10 minutes to blanch. Trim the root ends off each leek, being careful to keep the leeks intact. Trim the dark green tops off, then split the leeks lengthwise up to but not through the root. Rinse the leeks thoroughly, easing the leaves apart to remove the grit.

2. In a large bowl, combine the broth, soy sauce, ketchup, vinegar, sesame oil, and salt. Add the potatoes, leeks, and mushrooms, tossing well to coat. Set aside to marinate while the grill preheats.

3. Preheat the grill with the grill topper to a medium heat. Spray the grill topper—off the grill—with nonstick cooking spray (see page 6). Reserving the marinade, place the vegetables on the grill topper and grill, covered, turning occasionally, for 7 minutes or until the potatoes are tender.

4. Thickly slice the mushrooms and cut the potatoes into quarters. Cut the leeks into 1½-inch lengths and return them to the bowl along with the mushrooms and potatoes. Add the chopped parsley, tossing to combine. Serve warm or at room temperature.

Helpful hint: You can marinate the vegetables for up to 5 hours in the refrigerator.

FAT: 3G/13%
CALORIES: 215
SATURATED FAT: .3G
CARBOHYDRATE: 44G
PROTEIN: 6G
CHOLESTEROL: 0MG
SODIUM: 644MG

GRILLED RED ONIONS

SERVES: 4
WORKING TIME: 15 MINUTES
TOTAL TIME: 20 MINUTES

2 tablespoons sugar
1½ teaspoons ground ginger
1 teaspoon dried oregano
1 teaspoon salt
½ teaspoon ground allspice
½ teaspoon freshly ground black pepper
3 pounds large red onions, cut into ½-inch-thick rounds
¾ cup orange juice
1 tablespoon olive oil

1. Preheat the grill with the grill topper to a medium heat. (When ready to cook, spray the grill topper—off the grill—with non-stick cooking spray; see page 6.)

2. In a large bowl, combine the sugar, ginger, oregano, salt, allspice, and pepper. Add the onion rings, tossing well to coat. Add the orange juice and oil and toss again. Place the onions on the grill topper and grill, covered, turning occasionally, for 18 minutes or until the onions are crisp-tender. Serve hot.

Helpful hint: Any type of mild-to-sweet onion, such as Bermuda, Spanish, Vidalia, or Walla Walla, would also work well in this recipe.

FAT: 4G/16%
CALORIES: 220
SATURATED FAT: .5G
CARBOHYDRATE: 44G
PROTEIN: 6G
CHOLESTEROL: 0MG
SODIUM: 587MG

Lean *steaks are instantly transformed into a feast when you top them with these tangy spiced onions.*

That's right, there's a whole head of garlic in this recipe. But fear not, grilling the garlic tames its flavor to something that's savory, not savage. In fact, you can spread grilled garlic on bread or vegetables as a tastier, fat-free alternative to butter. Serve this bright carrot salad with grilled game hens or turkey breast.

GRILLED CARROT AND GARLIC SALAD

SERVES: 4
WORKING TIME: 15 MINUTES
TOTAL TIME: 45 MINUTES

2 pounds carrots, peeled
2 tablespoons fresh lemon juice
1 large or 2 small bulbs garlic, unpeeled
8 scallions, trimmed
1 teaspoon grated orange zest
1 cup orange juice
⅔ cup chopped fresh parsley
1 teaspoon salt
1 teaspoon ground cinnamon
1 teaspoon ground cumin
½ teaspoon ground ginger

1. Preheat the grill with the grill topper to a medium heat. (When ready to cook, spray the grill topper—off the grill—with nonstick cooking spray; see page 6.)

2. In a large pot of boiling water, cook the carrots for 7 minutes to blanch. Drain and toss with the lemon juice. Meanwhile, wrap the garlic bulb in a piece of foil. Place the carrots and scallions on the grill topper, and the garlic bulb on the grill rack and grill, covered, turning occasionally, for 6 minutes or until the carrots and scallions are tender. Remove the carrots and scallions from the grill and cook the garlic for 14 minutes longer or until soft.

3. Cut the carrots on the diagonal into 2-inch pieces, discarding the ends. Cut the scallions into 2-inch julienne strips. Unwrap the garlic, snip off the stem end, and squeeze the softened garlic out of the bulb (see tip) into a large bowl. Add the orange zest, orange juice, parsley, salt, cinnamon, cumin, and ginger, whisking to combine. Add the carrots and scallions and toss well. Serve warm, at room temperature, or chilled.

Helpful hint: To get a head start on dinner, you can blanch the carrots and toss them with the lemon juice up to 2 hours before you start the grill.

FAT: 1G/5%
CALORIES: 170
SATURATED FAT: .1G
CARBOHYDRATE: 39G
PROTEIN: 5G
CHOLESTEROL: 0MG
SODIUM: 635MG

TIP

To extract the cooked, sweet garlic pulp from the whole bulb of garlic, snip off the top of the bulb with kitchen scissors. Gently squeeze the sides of the bulb to force the cooked pulp out of the cloves and add it to the bowl.

ASPARAGUS PARMESAN

SERVES: 4
WORKING TIME: 15 MINUTES
TOTAL TIME: 30 MINUTES

2 pounds thick asparagus, tough ends trimmed

¼ cup reduced-sodium chicken broth, defatted

½ teaspoon grated lemon zest

½ teaspoon dried thyme

½ teaspoon salt

3 tablespoons grated Parmesan cheese

1. Preheat the grill with the grill topper to a medium heat. (When ready to cook, spray the grill topper—off the grill—with nonstick cooking spray; see page 6.)

2. Tear off a 30-inch length of heavy-duty foil and fold in half to form a 15 x 18-inch rectangle. Place the asparagus in the center of the foil. Fold the edges of the foil up a bit to form a lip and pour in the broth. Sprinkle with the lemon zest, thyme, and salt and seal the packet (see page 8).

3. Grill the packet on the grill topper, covered, for 12 minutes or until just crisp-tender. Carefully open the packet and, using tongs, transfer the asparagus to the grill topper. Grill, covered, for 3 minutes or until lightly browned. Transfer to a platter, sprinkle with the Parmesan, and serve.

Helpful hint: Thicker asparagus often benefit from having the tough skin on the lower part of the stalk peeled off. Use a swivel-bladed vegetable peeler to remove the peel from the bottom half of the stalks after trimming the tough, white ends.

FAT: 2G/29%
CALORIES: 61
SATURATED FAT: .8G
CARBOHYDRATE: 7G
PROTEIN: 7G
CHOLESTEROL: 3MG
SODIUM: 387MG

While asparagus may seem like an unlikely candidate for grilling, pre-steaming the delicate spears keeps them plump and juicy. For this initial step, the asparagus is cooked with broth, lemon, and thyme in a foil packet which infuses the vegetable with flavor. Garnish this delectable side dish with lemon and serve with grilled fresh fish and herbed potatoes.

Grilled Peppers

SERVES: 4
WORKING TIME: 20 MINUTES
TOTAL TIME: 30 MINUTES

These fire-roasted peppers are one of the great pleasures of grilling. Excellent just as they are, they're even better when bathed in a savory herbed dressing as we do here. You can toss them with hot pasta, lavish them on chicken breasts or swordfish steaks, or heap them on toasted rolls. They can also be used in any recipe that calls for roasted peppers from a jar.

2 cloves garlic, unpeeled

4 bell peppers, mixed colors, halved lengthwise and seeded

2 anchovy fillets or ½ teaspoon anchovy paste (optional)

½ teaspoon firmly packed light or dark brown sugar

3 tablespoons balsamic vinegar

1 teaspoon olive oil

¼ cup chopped fresh basil

1. Preheat the grill to a medium heat. Spray the rack—off the grill—with nonstick cooking spray (see page 6). Wrap the garlic cloves in a piece of foil. Grill the garlic packet and the pepper halves, cut-sides up, covered, without turning, for 10 minutes or until the pepper skins are blackened. Remove the peppers from the grill. When cool enough to handle, peel the peppers and cut them into ½-inch-wide strips.

2. Continue grilling the garlic for 10 minutes or until softened. When cool enough to handle, snip the stem end of each clove of garlic and squeeze the garlic pulp into a large bowl. Add the anchovies, mashing until well combined. Whisk in the brown sugar, vinegar, and oil. Add the peppers and basil to the bowl, toss well, and serve warm, at room temperature, or chilled.

Helpful hint: If the wires of your grill are widely spaced, be sure to wrap the garlic cloves in a large enough piece of foil so that they won't fall through.

FAT: 1G/24%
CALORIES: 38
SATURATED FAT: .1G
CARBOHYDRATE: 7G
PROTEIN: 2G
CHOLESTEROL: 1MG
SODIUM: 76MG

L*ike all chili peppers, jalapeños take on a whole new dimension when roasted over an open fire. Combine them with grilled bell peppers, tomatoes, and scallions and you're headed for the finest salsa ever. If you can save some before it's all scooped up (with low-fat tortilla chips or oven-baked tortilla triangles), try it on burgers and baked potatoes, too.*

GRILLED TOMATO SALSA

SERVES: 4
WORKING TIME: 15 MINUTES
TOTAL TIME: 25 MINUTES

2 green bell peppers, halved lengthwise and seeded, membranes removed

2 jalapeño peppers, halved lengthwise and seeded (see tip)

2 pounds firm-ripe tomatoes

4 scallions, trimmed

⅓ cup chopped fresh cilantro or parsley

3 tablespoons red wine vinegar

1 teaspoon olive oil

1 teaspoon ground cumin

1 teaspoon salt

1. Preheat the grill with the grill topper to a medium heat. Spray the grill topper—off the grill—with nonstick cooking spray (see page 6). Grill the bell peppers and the jalapeños on the grill topper, cut-sides up, covered, for 10 minutes or until blackened. Remove from the grill and set aside. Grill the tomatoes, stem-sides up, on the grill topper, covered, for 8 minutes or until they blister, char, and soften. Remove from the grill and set aside. Grill the scallions on the grill topper, covered, for 2 minutes or until lightly browned.

2. Peel the bell peppers. Coarsely chop the bell peppers, jalapeños, and the tomatoes, with their skins, and transfer to a large bowl. Slice the scallions and add to the bowl along with the cilantro, vinegar, oil, cumin, and salt. Serve at room temperature.

Helpful hint: Use tomatoes that are firm-ripe—ripe so the flavor is at its peak, yet firm so the tomatoes won't fall apart on the grill.

FAT: 2G/22%
CALORIES: 81
SATURATED FAT: .3G
CARBOHYDRATE: 15G
PROTEIN: 3G
CHOLESTEROL: 0MG
SODIUM: 576MG

TIP

Most of the heat from fresh chili peppers comes from the volatile oils found in the ribs (and to a lesser extent in the seeds). For a tamer dish, omit those parts. When working with chili peppers, fresh or grilled, use rubber gloves to protect your hands and keep your hands away from your face, especially the eyes. Wash your hands thoroughly with hot soapy water when you're done.

GRILLED POTATOES AND SWEET POTATOES

SERVES: 4
WORKING TIME: 20 MINUTES
TOTAL TIME: 35 MINUTES

These thick but tender potato slices can be likened to steakhouse fries: The difference is that these are grilled with a minimum of oil, rather than immersed in deep fat. Their garlic and rosemary seasonings also set them apart from everyday potatoes. Partner them with lamb chops or flank steak.

2 baking potatoes (8 ounces each)
2 sweet potatoes (8 ounces each)
2 cloves garlic, peeled and halved
¼ cup reduced-sodium chicken broth, defatted
2 teaspoons olive oil
½ teaspoon dried rosemary
½ teaspoon salt

1. Preheat the grill to a medium heat. (When ready to cook, spray the rack—off the grill—with nonstick cooking spray; see page 6.)

2. In a large pot of boiling water, cook the baking potatoes and sweet potatoes until almost tender, about 15 minutes. When cool enough to handle, slice the potatoes lengthwise into ½-inch-thick slices. Rub the potatoes with the garlic cloves. In a shallow bowl, combine the broth, oil, and rosemary. Add the potatoes, tossing to coat.

3. Grill the potatoes, covered, turning occasionally, for 10 minutes or until crisp outside and tender inside. Sprinkle with the salt and serve.

Helpful hint: Both sweet and white potatoes should be stored at cool, but not cold, temperatures. Do not keep them in the refrigerator as sweet potatoes will turn bland and white potatoes will develop an unappealing sweetness.

FAT: 2G/8%
CALORIES: 227
SATURATED FAT: .3G
CARBOHYDRATE: 49G
PROTEIN: 5G
CHOLESTEROL: 0MG
SODIUM: 260MG

GRILLED BUTTERNUT SQUASH

SERVES: 4
WORKING TIME: 15 MINUTES
TOTAL TIME: 30 MINUTES

Perfect *with turkey or pork, these hefty half-rounds of winter squash are coated with a bit of sugar and spice.*

2 tablespoons firmly packed light brown sugar

3 tablespoons fresh lime juice

½ teaspoon ground ginger

½ teaspoon salt

1 large butternut squash (2 pounds), halved lengthwise, peeled, and seeded

1. Preheat the grill with the grill topper to a medium heat. In a small bowl, combine the brown sugar, lime juice, ginger, and salt. Set aside.

2. Cut the squash crosswise into ½-inch-thick slices. Tear off a 30-inch length of heavy-duty foil, fold in half to form a 15 x 18-inch rectangle, and spray with nonstick cooking spray. Spread the squash on the foil in a double layer, sprinkle the brown sugar mixture on top, and seal the packet (see page 8).

3. Grill the packet on the rack (not the grill topper), covered, for 15 minutes or until the squash is almost tender. Spray the grill topper—off the grill—with nonstick cooking spray (see page 6). Carefully open the packet. Using tongs, transfer the squash to the grill topper, reserving the juices in the packet. Grill, covered, turning occasionally and basting with the reserved cooking juices, for 8 minutes or until browned and tender.

Helpful hint: You can cut up the squash and prepare the brown sugar mixture up to 8 hours in advance and keep them refrigerated separately until you are ready to assemble the packets.

FAT: 1G/8%
CALORIES: 119
SATURATED FAT: 0G
CARBOHYDRATE: 30G
PROTEIN: 2G
CHOLESTEROL: 0MG
SODIUM: 284MG

DESSERTS

5

Each grilled peach half is like an individual fruit crisp: The hollows in the peaches overflow with a buttery, cinnamon-laced mixture of oats, almonds, and brown sugar. Almonds and peaches are related botanically, so perhaps that's why their flavors complement each other particularly well.

GRILLED STUFFED PEACHES

SERVES: 4
WORKING TIME: 10 MINUTES
TOTAL TIME: 25 MINUTES

4 large peaches
2 tablespoons fresh lemon juice
⅓ cup quick-cooking oats
2 tablespoons firmly packed light brown sugar
1 tablespoon finely chopped almonds
1 tablespoon unsalted butter, melted
½ teaspoon cinnamon

1. In a large pot of boiling water, cook the peaches for 30 seconds to blanch (see tip; top photo). Rinse them under cold water and carefully remove their skins (bottom photo). With a sharp knife, halve and pit the peaches and cut a very thin slice from the back of each peach half so it will lie flat on the grill topper. In a medium bowl, toss the peach halves with the lemon juice.

2. Preheat the grill and the grill topper to a medium heat. (When ready to cook, spray the grill topper—off the grill—with nonstick cooking spray; see page 6.)

3. Meanwhile, in a small bowl, combine the oats, brown sugar, almonds, melted butter, and cinnamon. Dividing evenly, fill the centers of each peach half with the topping. Place the filled peach halves on the grill topper and cook, covered, for 5 to 6 minutes or until the peaches are tender. Place the peach halves on 4 plates and serve hot or warm.

Helpful hint: Almost all the peaches on the market today are freestones—that is, peaches whose pits can be easily removed. Some older peach varieties, which you may find at orchards and farm stands, are clingstones; though delicious for eating whole, they are difficult to use in a recipe calling for halved, pitted fruit.

FAT: 5G/28%
CALORIES: 161
SATURATED FAT: 2G
CARBOHYDRATE: 31G
PROTEIN: 3G
CHOLESTEROL: 8MG
SODIUM: 4MG

TIP

Place the peaches in a medium saucepan of boiling water and cook for 30 seconds to blanch. This will help loosen the skins without cooking the fruit. With a sharp paring knife, carefully pull away the skin and discard.

MIXED FRUIT KEBABS

SERVES: 4
WORKING TIME: 35 MINUTES
TOTAL TIME: 35 MINUTES

2 tablespoons honey
2 tablespoons orange juice
⅛ teaspoon nutmeg
4 cups mixed fresh fruit, cut into bite-sized chunks, such as pineapple, strawberries, apricots, nectarines, peaches, pears, and pitted whole cherries
2 teaspoons grated lime zest (optional)

1. Preheat the grill to a medium heat. (When ready to cook, spray the rack—off the grill—with nonstick cooking spray; see page 6.)

2. Meanwhile, in a large bowl, combine the honey, orange juice, and nutmeg. Add the fruit and toss to coat. Alternately thread the fruit onto 4 skewers.

3. Grill the kebabs, turning once, for 4 to 5 minutes or until the fruit is tender. Sprinkle with the lime zest and serve.

Helpful hint: You can skewer the fruits up to 30 minutes in advance: Prepare them before you sit down to dinner so they'll be ready to cook when it's time for dessert.

FAT: 1G/8%
CALORIES: 109
SATURATED FAT: 0G
CARBOHYDRATE: 28G
PROTEIN: 1G
CHOLESTEROL: 0MG
SODIUM: 1MG

One of the hallmarks of a good cook is the ability to adapt a recipe to the varying seasons, and this recipe encourages that kind of flexibility. Experiment with different combinations of seasonal fruits. Use local fruits if possible: Since they don't have to withstand the rigors of shipping, they're usually allowed to ripen longer and are often sweeter.

GRILLED ANGEL FOOD CAKE WITH CHOCOLATE SAUCE

SERVES: 4
WORKING TIME: 15 MINUTES
TOTAL TIME: 25 MINUTES

Sweet, light, and handsome though it is, angel food cake contains not a speck of fat: It's made without egg yolks or shortening. The perfect starting point for this healthy dessert, store-bought angel food cake is brushed with an orange-apricot glaze, toasted on the grill, and topped with a deceptively creamy milk chocolate sauce made with fat-free evaporated skim milk.

¼ cup apricot or orange spreadable fruit

3 tablespoons fresh orange juice

11-ounce prepared angel food cake

¼ cup evaporated skimmed milk

2 tablespoons semisweet chocolate chips (1 ounce)

2 tablespoons firmly packed light brown sugar

1 tablespoon unsweetened cocoa powder

½ teaspoon vanilla extract

1. Preheat the grill to a medium heat. (When ready to cook, spray the rack—off the grill—with nonstick cooking spray; see page 6.)

2. Meanwhile, in a small bowl, combine the spreadable fruit and orange juice. Quarter the angel food cake and cut each quarter in half horizontally to make 8 pieces of cake. Brush half of the fruit mixture on the cut sides of the cake pieces. Set aside.

3. Combine the evaporated milk, chocolate chips, brown sugar, cocoa powder, and vanilla in a small saucepan and cook directly on the grill or on the stovetop over medium heat until the sauce is smooth and slightly thickened, about 3 minutes. Remove from the heat.

4. Grill the cake, fruit-sides up, for 1 to 2 minutes or until browned. Turn the cake over, brush with the remaining fruit mixture, and grill for 1 to 2 minutes or until golden brown on the second side. Divide the cake among 4 plates, drizzle with the chocolate sauce, and serve.

Helpful hint: You can substitute another type of plain, fat-free cake for the angel food; if it's a loaf-shaped cake rather than a ring, cut it into eight ½-inch-thick slices.

FAT: 2G/6%
CALORIES: 317
SATURATED FAT: 1.1G
CARBOHYDRATE: 70G
PROTEIN: 6G
CHOLESTEROL: 1MG
SODIUM: 605MG

Hot Strawberry Sundaes

SERVES: 4
WORKING TIME: 20 MINUTES
TOTAL TIME: 30 MINUTES

What a spectacular combination: Jewel-like grilled strawberries in a warm orange sauce, spooned over vanilla frozen yogurt (peach yogurt would also be delicious). For an added note of sophistication, stir a teaspoon of orange liqueur, such as Cointreau, into the sauce along with the strawberries.

¼ cup orange juice
¼ cup strawberry spreadable fruit
1 teaspoon cornstarch
2 pints strawberries, hulled
2 cups low-fat vanilla frozen yogurt

1. Preheat the grill to a medium heat. (When ready to cook, spray the rack—off the grill—with nonstick cooking spray; see page 6.)

2. In a medium saucepan, combine the orange juice, strawberry spreadable fruit, and cornstarch. Set aside. Thread the strawberries onto 4 skewers.

3. Grill the kebabs, turning once, for 4 to 5 minutes. Meanwhile, place the medium saucepan directly on the grill or on the stovetop over medium heat and bring to a boil, stirring constantly. Cook, stirring, until the sauce is slightly thickened, about 1 minute.

4. Remove the strawberries from the skewers and stir into the sauce mixture in the saucepan. Cook until the mixture returns to a boil, 1 to 2 minutes. Divide the yogurt among 4 bowls, spoon the strawberry sauce over, and serve.

Helpful hints: This sauce is most impressive when served hot, but it's also good at room temperature or chilled. It could also be spooned over angel food cake that has been topped with nonfat vanilla yogurt for an extra-special "shortcake."

FAT: 2G/9%
CALORIES: 190
SATURATED FAT: 1G
CARBOHYDRATE: 41G
PROTEIN: 4G
CHOLESTEROL: 5MG
SODIUM: 62MG

DOUBLE CHOCOLATE S'MORES

SERVES: 4
WORKING TIME: 10 MINUTES
TOTAL TIME: 15 MINUTES

This update of the cookout favorite is made with low-fat cocoa sauce and just a small amount of chocolate chips.

¼ cup unsweetened cocoa powder

3 tablespoons firmly packed light brown sugar

2 tablespoons evaporated low-fat milk

8 graham crackers (2½-inch squares)

2 ounces mini chocolate chips

16 marshmallows

1. In a small bowl, combine the cocoa powder and brown sugar. Add the evaporated milk, stirring until the mixture is moistened and thick but not runny. Dividing evenly, spread the cocoa mixture over one side of each of the graham crackers. Sprinkle the chocolate chips onto 4 of the graham crackers. Place 4 marshmallows on each of the 4 chocolate-sprinkled graham crackers. Top with the remaining graham crackers, cocoa-sides down.

2. Preheat the grill to a medium heat.

3. Tear off four 6-inch lengths of heavy-duty foil, fold each in half to form a 9 x 6-inch rectangle, and spray with nonstick cooking spray. Place 1 s'more in the center of each rectangle and seal the packets (see page 8). Grill the packets for 4 minutes or until the marshmallows have melted.

Helpful hint: Double or even triple the recipe for a crowd of kids or a party.

FAT: 7G/22%
CALORIES: 282
SATURATED FAT: 3.1G
CARBOHYDRATE: 57G
PROTEIN: 4G
CHOLESTEROL: 1MG
SODIUM: 112MG

GRILLED BANANAS WITH RUM SAUCE

SERVES: 4
WORKING TIME: 15 MINUTES
TOTAL TIME: 15 MINUTES

4 large bananas (8 ounces each), unpeeled

⅔ cup firmly packed light brown sugar

½ cup fresh lime juice

¼ cup dark rum

¼ teaspoon ground allspice

¼ teaspoon nutmeg

1. Preheat the grill to a medium heat. Spray the grill rack—off the heat—with nonstick cooking spray (see page 6). Grill the bananas, covered, turning occasionally, for 6 minutes or until they are blackened. When cool enough to handle, slit the banana skins with a paring knife and carefully peel off. Cut the bananas on the diagonal into ½-inch slices.

2. Meanwhile, in a medium saucepan, combine the brown sugar, lime juice, and rum. Place the saucepan directly on the grill or on the stovetop over medium heat and bring to a gentle boil. Stir in the allspice and nutmeg. Add the sliced bananas to the rum sauce and cook, spooning the sauce over the bananas, until piping hot and well coated, about 3 minutes. Spoon the bananas onto 4 plates and serve.

Helpful hint: Use bananas that are ripe but still firm, so they don't fall apart when cooked.

FAT: 1G/3%
CALORIES: 316
SATURATED FAT: .3G
CARBOHYDRATE: 73G
PROTEIN: 2G
CHOLESTEROL: 0MG
SODIUM: 16MG

This tropical finale features bananas and rum—a heavenly combination. Use a dark rum for a more potent flavor.

143

OPEN-FACE PLUM TARTS

SERVES: 4
WORKING TIME: 25 MINUTES
TOTAL TIME: 25 MINUTES

If you've never tried backyard baking, this is a good recipe to start with. These charming tartlets couldn't be easier to prepare, but they look quite special —like something you'd be served at a French country inn. Using flour tortillas instead of pastry crust is the secret to their simplicity.

Four 6-inch flour tortillas
⅓ cup apple jelly
4 large red and/or green plums, thinly sliced
1 tablespoon sugar
½ teaspoon cinnamon

1. Preheat the grill with the grill topper to a medium heat. (When ready to cook, spray the grill topper—off the grill—with nonstick cooking spray; see page 6.)

2. Brush each tortilla with 2 teaspoons of the apple jelly. Arrange the sliced plums in concentric circles on each of the tortillas. (If using 2 different colors of plum, alternate the colors.) In a small bowl, combine the sugar and cinnamon and sprinkle over the plums.

3. Grill the tortillas on the grill topper, covered, for 6 to 7 minutes or until the plums are tender. Divide the tortillas among 4 plates, brush the remaining apple jelly over the hot plums and serve.

Helpful hint: This is a perfect recipe for children to help with. Place each tortilla on a plate and let the kids add the plum topping. The plates will also make it easier for you to slip the tarts onto the grill topper with little risk of a mishap.

FAT: 2G/9%
CALORIES: 193
SATURATED FAT: .3G
CARBOHYDRATE: 43G
PROTEIN: 3G
CHOLESTEROL: 0MG
SODIUM: 105MG

These grill-baked, fruit-and-nut-filled apples are just the thing to serve after a richer-than-usual meal. They're delicious the next day as well, should you be lucky enough to end up with leftovers: An apple half and a slice of whole wheat toast would make a delightful breakfast.

APPLES WITH APRICOT-NUT STUFFING

SERVES: 4
WORKING TIME: 35 MINUTES
TOTAL TIME: 35 MINUTES

4 large apples, cored and peeled

3 tablespoons fresh lemon juice

2 tablespoons apricot spreadable fruit

2 tablespoons chopped dried apricots

1 tablespoon finely chopped walnuts

1. Cut each apple in half lengthwise and then cut a thin slice from the back of each apple half (see tip). In a medium bowl, toss the apple halves with 2 tablespoons of the lemon juice.

2. Preheat the grill to a medium heat. In a small bowl, combine the spreadable fruit, chopped apricots, walnuts, and the remaining 1 tablespoon lemon juice.

3. Tear off two 24-inch lengths of heavy-duty foil, fold each in half to form a 12 x 18-inch rectangle, and spray with nonstick cooking spray. Place 4 apple halves in the center of each rectangle. Dividing evenly, spoon the apricot-nut stuffing into each apple half and seal the packets (see page 8).

4. Grill the packets for 8 to 10 minutes or until the apples are tender. Serve hot, warm, or at room temperature.

Helpful hint: If you don't have any lemons on hand, you can substitute orange juice for the lemon juice.

FAT: 2G/14%
CALORIES: 133
SATURATED FAT: .2G
CARBOHYDRATE: 31G
PROTEIN: 1G
CHOLESTEROL: 0MG
SODIUM: 1MG

TIP

With a sharp knife, cut each cored apple in half lengthwise. Cut a very thin slice from the rounded side of each half, creating a flat surface for the apple half to rest on while grilling.

GRILLED PINEAPPLE WITH ORANGE-MAPLE SAUCE

SERVES: 4
WORKING TIME: 30 MINUTES
TOTAL TIME: 30 MINUTES

1 small pineapple
¾ cup firmly packed dark brown sugar
3 tablespoons maple syrup
2 tablespoons fresh lime juice
½ teaspoon grated orange zest
⅓ cup fresh orange juice
2 tablespoons finely chopped pecans

1. Preheat the grill to a medium heat. (When ready to cook, spray the rack—off the grill—with nonstick cooking spray; see page 6.)

2. Meanwhile, with a large sharp knife, trim off the top and bottom of the pineapple. Cut the unpeeled pineapple crosswise into 8 rings (about ¾-inch thick). With an apple corer, sharp knife, or a small biscuit cutter, cut the tough center core out of the pineapple rings. In a small skillet, combine the brown sugar, maple syrup, and lime juice. Brush the pineapple rings with 2 tablespoons of the brown sugar mixture and grill the pineapple, covered, turning occasionally, for 6 minutes or until golden brown.

3. Meanwhile, add the orange zest and orange juice to the brown sugar mixture remaining in the skillet. Place the skillet directly on the grill or on the stovetop over medium heat and bring to a boil. Cook until slightly thickened and syrupy, about 4 minutes.

4. Place the pineapple rings on 4 plates, top with the orange-maple sauce, sprinkle with the pecans, and serve.

Helpful hint: You can prepare the whole dessert in advance, but don't sprinkle on the nuts until just before serving.

Fresh pineapple is always a treat—even more so when it's grilled with a citrusy maple basting sauce. Leaving the rind on the pineapple slices helps keep them intact on the grill and also conserves their juices. A topping of chopped pecans is the perfect finishing touch.

FAT: 3G/9%
CALORIES: 293
SATURATED FAT: .2G
CARBOHYDRATE: 70G
PROTEIN: 1G
CHOLESTEROL: 0MG
SODIUM: 19MG

If
fall weather brings the
grilling season to a
close in your part of
the country, be sure to
try this recipe before
you put your
equipment away for
the winter. Pears are
plentiful in the
autumn, and the
toasty taste of
butterscotch is just the
thing for a chilly-day
dessert.

GRILLED PEARS WITH BUTTERSCOTCH SAUCE

SERVES: 4
WORKING TIME: 25 MINUTES
TOTAL TIME: 25 MINUTES

4 large firm-ripe Anjou or Bartlett pears
3 tablespoons fresh lime juice
2 tablespoons granulated sugar
⅓ cup evaporated skimmed milk
2 tablespoons firmly packed light brown sugar
2 teaspoons unsalted butter
½ teaspoon vanilla extract

1. Preheat the grill and the grill topper to a medium heat. (When ready to cook, spray the rack—off the grill—with nonstick cooking spray; see page 6.)

2. Peel the pears, halve them lengthwise, and core (see tip). With a sharp knife, cut a very thin slice from the rounded side of each pear half so it will lie flat on the grill topper. In a medium bowl, toss the pear halves with the lime juice and granulated sugar.

3. Grill the pear halves on the grill topper for 4 minutes. Turn the pears over, drizzle with any remaining lime juice mixture, and grill for 5 minutes or until tender.

4. Meanwhile, in a small saucepan, combine the evaporated milk, brown sugar, butter, and vanilla. Cook directly on the grill or on the stovetop over medium heat, stirring constantly, until the mixture comes to a gentle boil. Cook until the sauce is smooth and slightly thickened, about 2 minutes. Divide the pears among 4 plates, drizzle with the butterscotch sauce, and serve hot or warm.

Helpful hint: The grilled pear halves—without the butterscotch sauce—would be a wonderful accompaniment to grilled poultry.

FAT: 3G/13%
CALORIES: 211
SATURATED FAT: 1.3G
CARBOHYDRATE: 48G
PROTEIN: 3G
CHOLESTEROL: 6MG
SODIUM: 27MG

TIP

With a paring knife, peel the pear. Halve the pear lengthwise and use a knife (or a grapefruit spoon) to cut out the core.

GRILLED FRUIT COMPOTE

SERVES: 4
WORKING TIME: 15 MINUTES
TOTAL TIME: 35 MINUTES

Compote is often made of dried fruit, but this one uses only fresh summer fruits. Experiment with different combinations of fruit and feel free to substitute strawberries, raspberries, or blackberries for any of the fruits listed, if you like. Since the compote is so low in fat, splurge a little and serve it with crisp wafer cookies or over vanilla frozen yogurt.

4 cups mixed fruit, such as blueberries, pitted cherries, sliced nectarines, sliced plums, and sliced peaches

2 tablespoons frozen orange juice concentrate

2 tablespoons firmly packed light brown sugar

1. Preheat the grill to a medium heat. In a large bowl, combine the mixed fruit, orange juice concentrate, and brown sugar.

2. Tear off two 48-inch lengths of heavy-duty foil, fold each in half to form a 24 x 18-inch rectangle, and spray with nonstick cooking spray. Place half the fruit mixture in the center of each rectangle and seal the packets (see page 8). Grill the packets, rotating twice, for 12 to 15 minutes or until the fruits are tender.

3. Open the packets, divide the compote among 4 plates, and serve.

Helpful hint: You can mix the fruit, juice, and sugar about 1 hour in advance, but don't make up the packets until you're ready to grill them.

FAT: 1G/1%
CALORIES: 125
SATURATED FAT: .1G
CARBOHYDRATE: 31G
PROTEIN: 2G
CHOLESTEROL: 0MG
SODIUM: 5MG

GLOSSARY

Allspice—A dark, round, dried berry about the size of a peppercorn, called allspice because it tastes like a blend of cloves, cinnamon, and nutmeg. Usually sold in ground form, allspice is often mistakenly thought to be a mix of several spices.

Anchovy paste—A combination of mashed anchovies, vinegar, spices, and water, available in convenient tubes. It's a quick, easy way to infuse sauces and marinades with robust flavor and only minimal fat—if used sparingly.

Apricots, fresh and dried—A freestone fruit that resembles a small peach and has a sweet, floral flavor and fragrance. Fresh apricots are very perishable and don't ship well, so they are not always available. Buy those that seem ripest (tender and well colored, with no tinge of green). Keep them at room temperature for a few days to soften, if necessary, and refrigerate when ripe; use within two to three days. In their dried form, apricots are intensely flavored, perfect for low-fat cooking since their tartness compensates for the absence of higher-fat ingredients. Some dried apricots are treated with sulfur dioxide to preserve their color; the unsulphured variety is darker in color and richer in flavor. To plump dried apricots, soak them in warm water, orange juice, or brandy.

Arugula—A salad green with long, narrow leaves and an intriguing peppery flavor; also called rocket or roquette. Long a favorite in Italian communities, arugula has become widely popular in recent years. In addition to its use in salads, arugula can be lightly sautéed and served as a hot vegetable side dish. Choose tender arugula with crisp stems; store it in a plastic bag in the refrigerator.

Balsamic vinegar—A dark red vinegar made from the unfermented juice of pressed grapes, most commonly the white Trebbiano, and aged in wooden casks. The authentic version is produced in a small region in Northern Italy, around Modena, and tastes richly sweet with a slight sour edge. Because this vinegar is so mild, you can make dressings and marinades with less oil.

Basmati rice—An aromatic, long-grain rice with a nutty flavor and fragrance, available in both white and brown forms. It is the rice used in the finest Indian dishes. Grown primarily in northern India and Pakistan—but also in California and Texas—basmati rice can be found at Middle Eastern food shops or in the rice section of your supermarket.

Caper—The flower bud of a small bush found in Mediterranean countries. To make capers, the buds are dried and then pickled in a vinegar brine; to reduce the saltiness, rinse before using. The piquant taste of capers permeates any sauce quickly, and just a few supply a big flavor boost.

Cherries—A small, round tree fruit with sweet, juicy flesh and a single central pit. The most popular sweet cherry for eating fresh is the Bing—large, round, and deep-red with a particularly sweet flavor. Store cherries in the refrigerator, covered, for up to 4 days. Sour cherries, such as the Montmorency variety, are used for baking and cooking.

Chili powder—A commercially prepared seasoning mixture made from ground dried chilies, oregano, cumin, coriander, salt, and dehydrated garlic, and sometimes cloves and allspice; used in chilis, sauces, and spice rubs for a Southwestern punch. Chili powders can range in strength from mild to very hot; for proper potency, use within 6 months of purchase.

Cilantro/Coriander—A lacy-leaved green herb (called by both names). The plant's seeds are dried and used as a spice (known as coriander). The fresh herb, much used in Mexican and Asian cooking, looks like pale flat-leaf parsley and is strongly aromatic. Store fresh cilantro by placing the stems in a container of water and covering the leaves loosely with a plastic bag. Coriander seeds are important in Mexican and Indian cuisines; sold whole or ground, they have a somewhat citrusy flavor that complements both sweet and savory dishes.

Couscous—Fine granules of pasta made from semolina flour. Of North African origin, couscous is traditionally cooked by steaming it over boiling water or a pot of stew. The couscous sold in boxes in American markets is quick cooking ("instant"): It requires only a few minutes of steeping in boiling water or broth. Couscous can be served as a side dish, like rice, or used as the basis for a hearty main dish.

Cream cheese, reduced-fat—A light cream cheese, commonly called Neufchâtel, with about one-third less fat than regular cream cheese. It can be used as a substitute for regular cream cheese. A small amount used in baking or in sauces duplicates the richness of full-fat cheese or heavy cream.

Cumin—A pungent, peppery-tasting spice essential to many Middle Eastern, Asian, Mexican, and Mediterranean dishes. Available ground or as whole seeds; the spice can be toasted in a dry skillet to bring out its flavor.

Curry powder—Not one spice but a mix of spices, commonly used in Indian cooking to flavor a dish with sweet heat and add a characteristic yellow-orange color. While curry blends vary (consisting of as many as 20 herbs and spices), they typically include turmeric (for its vivid yellow color), fenugreek, ginger, cloves, cumin, coriander, and cayenne pepper. Commercially available Madras curry is hotter than other store-bought types.

Eggplant—An oval or pear-shaped, purple- or white-skinned vegetable with mild-flavored, porous flesh. The familiar large eggplants can be cut into thick "steaks" for grilling; slender Chinese or Japanese eggplants can simply be halved. Eggplant takes on a meaty flavor when cooked with savory ingredients; when fried, it soaks up a tremendous amount of oil, but grilling renders it smoky and delicious with no added fat.

Fennel seed—A seed from the fennel plant with a slightly sweet, licorice-like taste, often used to season Italian-style sausages. It's also particularly good with grilled fish.

Ginger, fresh—A thin-skinned root used as a seasoning. Fresh ginger adds sweet pungency to Asian and Indian dishes. Tightly wrapped, unpeeled fresh ginger can be refrigerated for 1 week or frozen for up to 6 months. Ground ginger is not a true substitute for fresh, but it will lend a warming flavor to soups, stews, and sauces.

Honey—A liquid sweetener made by honeybees from flower nectar. It ranges in flavor from mild (orange blossom) to very strong (buckwheat). Deliciously versatile, honey can sweeten savory sauces or serve as a glaze for grilled fruits. Store honey

at room temperature. If it crystallizes, place the open jar in a pan of warm water for a few minutes; or microwave it for 15 seconds, or until the honey liquifies.

Horseradish—A root vegetable used as a seasoning, sold whole or prepared (grated and mixed with vinegar). Horseradish is an ideal flavoring: Fat-free and low in sodium, it makes a lively addition to marinades and sauces. Freshly grated from the whole root, it has head-clearing pungency. Bottled prepared horseradish loses its potency with time, so if you have some on hand, check to see if it is still flavorful before using it. To store the fresh root, wrap well and refrigerate; peel before using.

Maple syrup—A liquid sweetener made by boiling down the sap of sugar maple trees. Not just sweet, maple syrup has a unique toasty fragrance and flavor that complement the taste of grilled foods. Pure maple syrup comes in a range of grades, the mildest and lightest being AA or Fancy; grades A and B are fine for cooking. In basting sauces and the like, honey or corn syrup can be substituted for maple syrup, although the flavor will of course be different. Once the container is opened, store maple syrup in the refrigerator; it should keep for up to a year.

Mint—A large family of herbs used to impart a refreshingly heady fragrance and cool aftertaste to foods; the most common types are spearmint and peppermint. As with other fresh herbs, mint is best added toward the end of the cooking time. Dried mint is fairly intense, so a pinch goes a long way. Store fresh mint the same way as fresh cilantro.

Mustard—A pungent seed used whole as a spice, or ground and mixed with other ingredients to form a paste. Mustard seeds come in a variety of colors, from white to yellow to brown to black, with flavors ranging from mild to hot. Pre-

pared mustard is made by combining the ground seeds with a liquid, often wine or vinegar. The Dijon type of prepared mustard is made with dry white wine and is often flavored with herbs such as tarragon. Prepared mustard is excellent in marinades, salad dressings, and in any dish where you want a bit of tang. It's also naturally fat free.

Napa cabbage—A member of the cabbage family, identified particularly with Chinese cooking. Napa cabbage has broad white ribs and frilly, light green leaves; it is slightly sweet, and much milder than regular cabbage. Look for heads with firm leaves and unbrowned edges. To store, refrigerate, unwashed, in a plastic bag for up to 1 week. Napa cabbage adds crunch and subtle green color to skillet or stir-fried dishes and salads.

Olive oil—A fragrant cooking oil pressed from olives. Olive oil is rich in monounsaturated fat, which is more healthful than the saturated fat found in butter and other solid shortenings. Olive oil comes in different grades, reflecting the method used to refine the oil and the resulting level of acidity. The finest, most expensive, oil is cold-pressed extra-virgin, which should be reserved for flavoring salad dressings and other uncooked or lightly cooked foods. Virgin and pure olive oils are slightly more acidic with less olive flavor, and are fine for most types of cooking.

Orzo—A small pasta shape that resembles large grains of rice. Orzo is popular in Greece and makes a delicious alternative to rice, especially with Mediterranean-inspired meals.

Parsley—A popular herb available in two varieties. Curly parsley, with lacy, frilly leaves, is quite mild and is preferred for garnishing, while flat-leaf Italian parsley has a stronger flavor and is better for cooking. Store parsley as you would cilantro. Since fresh parsley is so widely available, there is really no reason to use dried, which has little flavor.

Peach—A sweet summer tree fruit with a large central stone and fuzzy skin. Peaches may be freestone, semi-free-stone, or clingstone, but almost all peaches sold fresh in the supermarkets are freestone— the fruit can be halved and pitted very easily (clingstones, which have firmer flesh, are processed for canning). It's best to buy local peaches in season—they're picked closer to full ripeness so they'll be sweeter. When buying peaches that have been shipped from a distance, choose those that are not rock-hard and have a warm cream-to-yellow color with a rosy tinge. Keep them at room temperature until they yield to finger pressure and are sweetly fragrant.

Pecan—A native American nut that is equally at home in savory dishes and desserts. Pecans have the highest fat content of any nut, so they are highly perishable; store them in a sealed container in the refrigerator for up to 3 months, or in the freezer for up to 6 months.

Plum—A juicy, glossy-skinned tree fruit with a small central pit. Plums come in a wide variety of colors but just two basic types: Japanese plums are the plump, round clingstone varieties, such as Santa Rosa and Larodas, that are mostly eaten fresh. Italian plums (sometimes called prune plums) are the egg-shaped purple fruits that are tasty for eating fresh but are also excellent for cooking—they're freestone and therefore

easy to pit and slice. Purchase plums that are at least somewhat soft at the tip; leave them at room temperature for a few days to soften, then refrigerate.

Potatoes, small red—Diminutive versions of the waxy round red boiling potato, usually no larger than 1½ inches in diameter. These are sometimes mistakenly called "new potatoes"— which they may or may not be, depending on the season (the term "new" refers to any type of potato that has been freshly dug and has not been stored). Small white potatoes can be used instead.

Prune—Dried plums, eaten as a sweet snack or used as a cooking ingredient. Sold whole or pitted, prunes are an outstanding source of dietary fiber. If prunes become too dry, plump them by soaking them in hot water or fruit juice for a few minutes (or, sprinkle them with a little water or juice, cover, and microwave on high power for 2 minutes.)

Sage—An intensely fragrant herb with grayish-green leaves. An Italian favorite, sage will infuse a dish with a pleasant, musty mint taste; it's especially good with poultry and is often used in stuffings. In its dried form, sage is sold as whole leaves, ground, and in a fluffy "rubbed" version. For the best flavor from the dried herb, buy whole leaves and crush them yourself.

Sugar, brown—Granulated white sugar mixed with molasses for a softer texture and fuller flavor than plain white sugar. Dark brown sugar, made with more molasses, has a richer, sweeter flavor, although the two can be used interchangeably in recipes. To keep brown sugar soft, store in an airtight container with a slice of fresh bread.

Tarragon—A potent, sweet herb with a licorice- or anise-like flavor. Dried tarragon loses its potency quickly; check for flavor intensity by crushing a little between your fingers and sniffing for the strong aroma. As with most herbs, you may substitute 1 teaspoon dried for each tablespoon of fresh.

Tomatoes, cherry—Round tomatoes roughly the size of ping-pong balls; may be red or yellow. Cherry tomatoes are just the right size for kebabs and can also be sautéed, whole or halved, and, of course, used in salads. Cherry tomatoes are usually sold in baskets. Choose the reddest ones you can find and store them at room temperature to preserve their flavor.

Worcestershire sauce—A richly savory condiment based on vinegar, molasses, garlic, anchovies, tamarind, and onion. It takes its name from Worcester, England, where it was first bottled. Worcestershire is frequently used with meat—as a table condiment and in sauces or marinades. If the bottle is kept tightly capped, this potent condiment will keep almost indefinitely at room temperature.

Zest, citrus—The very thin, outermost colored part of the rind of citrus fruits that contains strongly flavored oils. Zest imparts an intense flavor that makes a refreshing contrast to the richness of meat, poultry, or fish. Used in marinades, it helps tenderize foods. Remove the zest with a grater, citrus zester, or vegetable peeler; be careful to scrape off only the colored layer, not the bitter white pith beneath it.

Zucchini—A delicately flavored summer squash that looks like a cucumber with a white-speckled skin. The golden version of this squash makes a pretty contrast when you're grilling a variety of vegetables; its flesh is more yellow than that of regular zucchini, but the flavor is about the same.

Index

Angel Food Cake, Grilled, with Chocolate Sauce, 139
Apples with Apricot-Nut Stuffing, 147
Asian Chicken and Broccoli Salad, 24
Asian Grilled Pork Salad, 47
Asparagus Parmesan, 124

Bananas, Grilled, with Rum Sauce, 143
Beef
    Apricot-Glazed Beef Kebabs, 69
    Beef Burgers with Basil and Mozzarella, 50
    Chili Burgers, 61
    Grilled Beef with Squash and Mushrooms, 48
    Grilled Beef with Tomato Salsa, 43
    Grilled Curried Beef, 60
    Grilled Flank Steak and Vegetable Salad, 54
    Herbed Cheeseburgers, 65
    Marinated Flank Steak and Potato Salad, 51
    Southwestern Beef Salad, 70
    Steak, Mushrooms, and Onions Burgundy, 57
Bluefish, Barbecued, with Grilled Potatoes, 97
Burgers. *See also Sandwiches*
    Beef Burgers with Basil and Mozzarella, 50
    Chili Burgers, 61
    Herbed Cheeseburgers, 65
    Italian-Style Turkey Burgers, 35
    Salmon Burgers, 100
Burritos, Vegetable, 105
Butternut Squash, Grilled, 132

Cake, Grilled Angel Food, with Chocolate Sauce, 139
Carrot and Garlic Salad, Grilled, 123
Charcoal-Grilled Turkey Breast with Stuffing, 37
Cheeseburgers, Herbed, 65
Chicken. *See also Game hens*
    Asian Chicken and Broccoli Salad, 24
    Barbecued Chicken with Tropical Fruit Salsa, 15
    Chicken Quesadillas, 32
    Chicken Souvlaki, 39
    Chicken with Red Chile Sauce, 31
    Dijon Chicken Kebabs, 17
    Grilled Buffalo Chicken Sandwiches, 21
    Grilled Chicken Fajitas, 23
    Moo Shu-Style Grilled Chicken, 19
    Old-Fashioned Texas Barbecued Chicken, 11
Chili Burgers, 61
Cod and Summer Vegetables in Packets, 94
Corn in the Husk, Grilled, 117
Cornish game hens. *See Game hens*

Desserts
    Apples with Apricot-Nut Stuffing, 147
    Double Chocolate S'Mores, 142
    Grilled Angel Food Cake with Chocolate Sauce, 139
    Grilled Bananas with Rum Sauce, 143
    Grilled Fruit Compote, 153
    Grilled Pears with Butterscotch Sauce, 151

    Grilled Pineapple with Orange-Maple Sauce, 148
    Grilled Stuffed Peaches, 135
    Hot Strawberry Sundaes, 141
    Mixed Fruit Kebabs, 136
    Open-Faced Plum Tarts, 145

Eggplant
    Grilled Eggplant "Caviar," 115
    Grilled Eggplant and Feta with Pasta, 109

Fajitas, Grilled Chicken, 23
Fish/shellfish
    Barbecued Bluefish with Grilled Potatoes, 97
    Barbecued Salmon with Plum Sauce, 92
    Cod and Summer Vegetables in Packets, 94
    Ginger-Soy Swordfish, 93
    Grilled Halibut with Fresh Tomato-Herb Sauce, 82
    Grilled Scallops with Thai Noodle Salad, 78
    Grilled Shrimp and Asparagus Salad, 89
    Grilled Trout with Fennel, 75
    Grilled Tuna Salad Niçoise, 86
    Herbed Flounder Rolls, 83
    Jamaican Jerked Shrimp with Pineapple, 81
    Mixed Seafood Kebabs with Parslied Pasta, 85
    Salmon Burgers, 100
    Salmon Steaks with Pesto and Peppers, 99
    Shrimp Kebabs with Lime-Basil Orzo, 73
    Striped Bass with Green Curry Sauce, 91
    Sweet and Sour Halibut, 77

Game hens
    Grilled Cornish Game Hens with Apples, 20
    Honey-Mustard Hens with Grilled Corn Salad, 27
    Spiced Cornish Game Hens, 40
Greek Lamb Kebabs with Mint Sauce, 53

Halibut
    Grilled Halibut with Fresh Tomato-Herb Sauce, 82
    Sweet and Sour Halibut, 77
Heros, Turkey Sausage and Pepper, 29

Italian-Style Turkey Burgers, 35

Jamaican Jerked Shrimp with Pineapple, 81

Kebabs
    Apricot-Glazed Beef Kebabs, 69
    Dijon Chicken Kebabs, 17
    Greek Lamb Kebabs with Mint Sauce, 53
    Mixed Fruit Kebabs, 136
    Mixed Seafood Kebabs with Parslied Pasta, 85
    Moroccan Lamb Kebabs, 45
    Shrimp Kebabs with Lime-Basil Orzo, 73
    Vegetable Kebabs, 119

Lamb
    Greek Lamb Kebabs with Mint Sauce, 53
    Moroccan Lamb Kebabs, 45

Meatless main courses
  Grilled Eggplant and Feta with Pasta,
    109
  Grilled Pizza, 106
  Grilled Vegetable and Mozzarella
    Sandwiches, 112
  Mixed Vegetable Packets, 103
  New Potato and Pepper Salad, 111
  Vegetable Burritos, 105
Moo Shu-Style Grilled Chicken, 19
Moroccan Lamb Kebabs, 45
Mushrooms
  Grilled Mushrooms, Potatoes, and
    Leeks, 120
  Grilled Stuffed Mushrooms, 114

Onions, Grilled Red, 121

Peaches, Grilled Stuffed, 135
Pears, Grilled, with Butterscotch Sauce,
  151
Peppers, Grilled, 127
Pineapple, Grilled, with Orange-Maple
  Sauce, 148
Pizza, Grilled, 106
Plum Tarts, Open-Faced, 145
Pork
  Asian Grilled Pork Salad, 47
  Grilled Honey-Mustard Pork Chops, 66
  Grilled Pork Tacos, 63
  Grilled Spiced Pork Chops with Chutney,
    59

Potatoes
  Grilled Mushrooms, Potatoes, and Leeks,
    120
  Grilled Potatoes and Sweet Potatoes, 131
  New Potato and Pepper Salad, 111

Quesadillas, Chicken, 32

Salads, main-course
  Asian Chicken and Broccoli Salad, 24
  Asian Grilled Pork Salad, 47
  Grilled Flank Steak and Vegetable Salad, 54
  Grilled Shrimp and Asparagus Salad, 89
  Grilled Tuna Salad Niçoise, 86
  Grilled Turkey and Orange Salad, 12
  New Potato and Pepper Salad, 111
  Southwestern Beef Salad, 70
Salads, side-dish
  Grilled Carrot and Garlic Salad, 123
Salmon
  Barbecued Salmon with Plum Sauce, 92
  Salmon Burgers, 100
  Salmon Steaks with Pesto and Peppers, 99
Salsa, Grilled Tomato, 129
Sandwiches
  Chicken Souvlaki, 39
  Chili Burgers, 61
  Grilled Buffalo Chicken Sandwiches, 21
  Grilled Vegetable and Mozzarella
    Sandwiches, 112
  Herbed Cheeseburgers, 65
  Italian-Style Turkey Burgers, 35

Steak, Mushrooms, and Onions Burgundy,
  57
Turkey Sausage and Pepper Heros, 29
Scallops
  Grilled Scallops with Thai Noodle Salad, 78
  Mixed Seafood Kebabs with Parslied
    Pasta, 85
Seafood. See Fish/shellfish
Shrimp
  Grilled Shrimp and Asparagus Salad, 89
  Jamaican Jerked Shrimp with Pineapple,
    81
  Mixed Seafood Kebabs with Parslied
    Pasta, 85
  Shrimp Kebabs with Lime-Basil Orzo, 73
S'Mores, Double Chocolate, 142
Southwestern Beef Salad, 70
Souvlaki, Chicken, 39
Squash, Grilled Butternut, 132
Steak
  Grilled Flank Steak and Vegetable Salad, 54
  Marinated Flank Steak and Potato Salad, 51
  Steak, Mushrooms, and Onions Burgundy,
    57
Strawberry Sundaes, Hot, 141
Striped Bass with Green Curry Sauce, 91
Sundaes, Hot Strawberry, 141
Sweet Potatoes, Grilled Potatoes and, 131
Swordfish
  Ginger-Soy Swordfish, 93
  Mixed Seafood Kebabs with Parslied
    Pasta, 85

Tacos, Grilled Pork, 63
Tarts, Open-Faced Plum, 145
Tomato Salsa, Grilled, 129
Trout, Grilled, with Fennel, 75
Tuna, Grilled, Salad Niçoise, 86
Turkey
  Charcoal-Grilled Turkey Breast with
    Stuffing, 37
  Grilled Turkey and Orange Salad, 12
  Italian-Style Turkey Burgers, 35
  Turkey Sausage and Pepper Heros, 29

Vegetables. See also Meatless main courses
Asparagus Parmesan, 124
Grilled Butternut Squash, 132
Grilled Carrot and Onion Salad, 123
Grilled Corn in the Husk, 117
Grilled Eggplant "Caviar," 115
Grilled Mushrooms, Potatoes, and
  Leeks, 120
Grilled Peppers, 127
Grilled Potatoes and Sweet Potatoes, 131
Grilled Red Onions, 121
Grilled Stuffed Mushrooms, 114
Grilled Tomato Salsa, 129
Vegetable Kebabs, 119